MW00389379

加油!
jiā yóu
Chinese for the Global Community
Workbook 1

许嘉璐 主编
XU Jialu

陈绂　　王若江　　朱瑞平
CHEN Fu　　WANG Ruojiang　　ZHU Ruiping

娄毅　　杨丽姣　　李凌艳　　Pedro ACOSTA
LOU Yi　　YANG Lijiao　　LI Lingyan

CENGAGE Learning™

北京师范大学出版集团
BEIJING NORMAL UNIVERSITY PUBLISHING GROUP
北京师范大学出版社

Chinese for the Global Community

Workbook 1 with Audio CDs

北京师范大学出版集团
BEIJING NORMAL UNIVERSITY PUBLISHING GROUP
北京师范大学出版社

Publishing Director/CLT Product Director: Paul Tan
Senior Development Editor: Lan Zhao
Associate Development Editor: Coco Koh
Graphic Designer: Debbie Ng
Assistant Publishing Manager: Pauline Lim
Product Manager (Outside Asia): Mei Yun Loh
Product Manager (Asia): Joyce Tan
Account Manager (China): Arthur Sun
CLT Coordinator (China): Mana Wu

Executive Editors: Fan Yang, Lili Yin
Graphic Designer: Baofen Li
Illustrator: Hai Bo
Proofreader: Han Li
Sound Engineers: Guangying Feng, Wei Wang, Shuai Wang
Sound Editor: Zhangji Wei

Cover and Layout Design: Redbean De Pte Ltd
Photos: Getty Images, unless otherwise stated

© 2008 Cengage Learning Asia Pte Ltd and Beijing Normal University Press

Printed in Singapore
4 5 6 7 8 9 10 — 13 12 11 10

ISBN: 978-981-4221-64-1 (International)
ISBN: 978-7-303-08419-7 (Mainland China)

For product information and orders, contact your local Cengage Learning or BNUP sales representatives.
Or visit our Websites at
www.cengageasia.com or **www.bnup.com.cn**
For permission to use material from this text or product, email to
asia.publishing@cengage.com

Cengage Learning products are represented in Canada by Nelson Education, Ltd.

CENGAGE LEARNING

Asia Head Office (Singapore)
Cengage Learning Asia Pte Ltd
5 Shenton Way #01-01
UIC Building
Singapore 068808
Tel: (65) 6410 1200
Fax: (65) 6410 1208
Email: asia.info@cengage.com

United States
Heinle, Cengage Learning
20 Channel Center Street
Boston, MA 02210
Tel: (1) 800 354 9706
    (1) 617 757 7900
Fax: (1) 800 487 8488

China
Cengage Learning Asia Pte Ltd
(Beijing Rep Office)
Room 1201, South Tower, Building C
Raycom Info Tech Park
No. 2, Kexueyuan South Road
Haidian District, Beijing, China 100080
Tel: (86) 10 8286 2096
Fax: (86) 10 8286 2089
Email: asia.infochina@cengage.com

Beijing Normal University Press

China
No. 19 Xinjiekouwai Street
Beijing, China 100875
Tel: (86) 10 5880 2833
Fax: (86) 10 5880 6196
Email: yll@bnup.com.cn
    fan@bnup.com.cn

Author's Message

Jia You! Chinese for the Global Community is specially written for anyone who seeks to learn about the Chinese culture and people, and to use this knowledge in the context of the global community.

The most important aim of learning another language is to be able to exchange ideas with people of another culture. In order to achieve this, you need to learn about the culture of the people you wish to communicate with. From this perspective, a good textbook should contain rich cultural content. It should also provide the learner with a variety of exercises and reference materials so that they can get more practice in using the language.

It was in accordance with the above principles that we wrote this textbook series. It was created by a team of distinguished Chinese and American scholars who are experts in both Chinese language teaching, and subjects such as educational psychology, Chinese history, and culture.

If you already have some knowledge of Chinese and would like to go on learning, then this textbook series is definitely suitable for you. We hope it will inspire you to lifelong learning about the Chinese language and people.

We are keen to hear feedback from students and teachers who use this textbook series. This will be of great help to us, and will also help in strengthening friendship between the Chinese and American people.

Xu Jialu

PRINCIPAL
College of Chinese Language and Culture
Beijing Normal University, China

Preface

The Workbook exercises are thematically linked to the content of each lesson, allowing students to apply newly-acquired vocabulary, sentence patterns, and cultural knowledge to new and meaningful tasks. The Workbook is a useful tool for assessing the student's grasp of the materials learned in the program and for furthering their communication and language skills.

The Workbook exercises can be used as instructional activities, as homework, or as timed assessments. The Workbook activities cover all four skills (listening, reading, writing, and speaking), three communicative modes (interpretive, interpersonal, and presentational), as well as cultural knowledge.

The Workbook format and question types are designed to resemble the AP Chinese Language and Culture exam; students taking the AP Chinese exam can therefore get extensive practice on the exam format. The Workbook can also be used by any intermediate student of Chinese who is looking for additional comprehensive language practice.

The exercises in each lesson are divided into two sections. Section One, which consists of multiple-choice questions, assesses the student on listening and reading comprehension. Section Two, which consists of free-response questions, assesses students on oral and written communication.

- **Listening Comprehension (Multiple Choice)** – There are two categories of listening exercises.

  ▶ The first category of listening exercises assesses interpersonal communication skills by requiring the student to listen to recordings of short conversations and then identify the appropriate continuation of each from a list of possible answers.

  ▶ The second category of listening exercises requires the student to listen to recordings of short Chinese texts in the form of announcements, conversations, instructions, broadcasts, messages or reports, and then answer multiple-choice questions about them. Students are allowed to take notes. These exercises assess interpretative communication skills; the student has to comprehend different forms of spoken Chinese, and identify main ideas and supporting details.

- **Reading Comprehension (Multiple-Choice)** – These exercises assess interpretative communication skills by requiring the student to answer questions about different types of reading texts (letters, notices, notes, signs, e-mails, or stories).

- **Writing (Free Response)** – The four questions in this section assess communication skills in the interpersonal and presentational modes by requiring the student to write in four different styles.

  ▶ Story Narration – The student has to produce a written narrative of a story as depicted by a series of pictures.

  ▶ Personal Letter – The student has to write a response to a letter from a pen pal, describing personal experiences, expressing preferences, and justifying opinions.

  ▶ E-Mail Response – The student has to read an e-mail from a friend and produce an appropriate written response.

  ▶ Relay a Telephone Message – The student has to listen to a voice telephone message and then relay the message by typing a note to a friend or family member.

- **Speaking (Free Response)** – The three questions in this section assess oral communication skills in the interpersonal and presentational modes.

  ▶ Simulated Conversation – The student has to respond orally to a series of thematically linked questions as part of a simulated conversation.

  ▶ Cultural Presentation – The student has to make an oral presentation describing and explaining the significance of a Chinese cultural practice or product.

  ▶ Event Plan – The student has to make an oral presentation on a plan for an event such as a fundraising fair, a three-day holiday trip, or an outdoor class activity.

Answer sheets for Section One multiple choice questions are provided at the end of the book. The Workbook comes with 3 audio CDs. The CDs provide the audio program for all listening activities.

Contents

UNIT ONE
LESSON 1
Sports and Fitness
Shaolin Kung Fu

Section One

I. Multiple Choice (Listen to the dialogs)

Note: In this part, you may NOT move back and forth among questions.

Directions: In this part, you will hear several short conversations or parts of conversations followed by four choices, designated (A), (B), (C), and (D). Choose the one that continues or completes the conversation in a logical and culturally appropriate manner. You will have 5 seconds to answer each question.

1.	(A)	(B)	(C)	(D)	5.	(A)	(B)	(C)	(D)
2.	(A)	(B)	(C)	(D)	6.	(A)	(B)	(C)	(D)
3.	(A)	(B)	(C)	(D)	7.	(A)	(B)	(C)	(D)
4.	(A)	(B)	(C)	(D)	8.	(A)	(B)	(C)	(D)

II. Multiple Choice (Listen to the selections)

Note: In this part, you may move back and forth only among the questions associated with the current listening selection.

Directions: In this part, you will listen to several selections in Chinese. For each selection, you will be told whether it will be played once or twice. You may take notes as you listen. After listening to each selection, you will see questions in English. For each question, choose the response that is best according to the selection. You will have 12 seconds to answer each question.

Selection 1

1. Why did the man call the sports center?
    (A) To ask about opening times of the sports center.
    (B) To ask about the usage fee for the badminton court.
    (C) To reserve a badminton court for the following day.
    (D) To ask about the location of the sports center.

2. When do the man and his friend plan to go to the sports center?

(A) 11:00 am   (B) 12:00 pm

(C) 7:00 pm   (D) 9:00 am

3. Which of these things does the woman say will affect the fee?

(A) The number of people booking the court.

(B) The amount of time spent there.

(C) The time of a day – it's more expensive in the evenings.

(D) The day of the week – it's more expensive on weekends.

4. How much money does the man need to pay?

(A) 50 *yuan*   (B) 100 *yuan*

(C) 150 *yuan*   (D) 200 *yuan*

Selection 2

5. If the sports meet is held as scheduled, when should it start?

(A) 8:00 am   (B) 8:30 am

(C) 8:45 am   (D) 9:00 am

6. Where will the sports meet be held?

(A) At the northern sports ground.

(B) At the eastern sports ground.

(C) At the western sports ground.

(D) At the southern sports ground.

Selection 3

7. What are the two people talking about?

(A) Yao Ming's basketball skills.

(B) Yao Ming's basketball team.

(C) Yao Ming's photo.

(D) Yao Ming's fans.

8. According to this conversation, which of the following statements is TRUE?

(A) The man watched Yao Ming play in Shanghai.

(B) Yao Ming played in Shanghai in January.

(C) Xiao Ling watched Yao Ming play in Shanghai.

(D) The man wants to get a photo from Xiao Ling.

Selection 4

9. Why was Xiao Wang in a bad mood today?
    (A) Because he lost a game yesterday.
    (B) Because he missed a game yesterday.
    (C) Because his favorite team lost a game.
    (D) Because he could not take part in the final game.

10. Which team does Xiao Wang like?
    (A) Brazil   (B) England
    (C) The USA   (D) Italy

11. According to the conversation, which of the following statements is TRUE?
    (A) The woman likes soccer as much as the man.
    (B) The soccer game last night was the final.
    (C) The woman didn't watch the soccer game last night.
    (D) The woman's favorite soccer team is Brazil.

Selection 5

12. What day is the game on?
    (A) This coming Wednesday   (B) This coming Monday
    (C) The following Wednesday   (D) The following Monday

13. Does Xiao Zhang think it will be easy to buy tickets?
    (A) Yes, he thinks it will be easy.
    (B) No, he thinks it will be difficult.
    (C) Yes, he knows someone who can help him.
    (D) No, he thinks it will be impossible.

14. What does Xiao Zhang hope Li Bing will do as soon as possible?
    (A) Buy tickets at the stadium.
    (B) Watch the game at the stadium.
    (C) Give him a call.
    (D) Buy him a ticket.

15. What kind of ticket does Xiao Zhang hope to buy?
    (A) The cheapest tickets.
    (B) Tickets for good seats.
    (C) The same ticket as Li Bing's.
    (D) Tickets for the seats nearest to the field.

III. Multiple Choice (Reading)

Note: In this part, you may move back and forth among all the questions.

Directions: You will read several selections in Chinese. Each selection is accompanied by a number of questions in English. For each question, choose the response that is best according to the selection.

Read this e-mail.

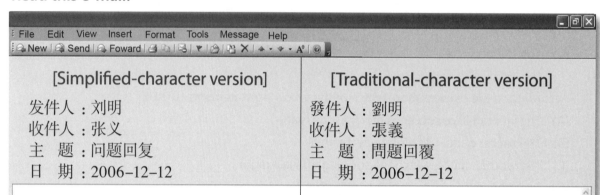

[Simplified-character version]	[Traditional-character version]
发件人：刘明	發件人：劉明
收件人：张义	收件人：張義
主　题：问题回复	主　題：問題回覆
日　期：2006–12–12	日　期：2006–12–12

张义：

　　你好！关于你上次问的问题，我找到了有关的资料。

　　中国象棋，古代叫"象戏"。大约起源于战国时代，是一种根据两军作战的情况创造的游戏。唐朝时，象棋已经很普及，到了宋代，中国象棋更加完善，并且在全国流行起来。中国象棋的棋盘是正方形的，棋盘的中间有一条"界河"，双方各占一边。中国象棋共有32个棋子，分为黑红两组，下棋的双方各用一组。各种棋子的走法不同。两人下棋时，红方先走，然后轮流下棋子。当一方失去了做统帅的棋子时，另一方就赢了。当然也有不分胜负的时候，那就是和棋。1949年以后，中国象棋成为全国正式体育比赛项目之一。

　　希望这些内容可以回答你的问题。
　　祝
工作顺利！

刘明

張義：

　　你好！關於你上次問的問題，我找到了有關的資料。

　　中國象棋，古代叫"象戲"。大約起源於戰國時代，是一種根據兩軍作戰的情況創造的遊戲。唐朝時，象棋已經很普及，到了宋代，中國象棋更加完善，並且在全國流行起來。中國象棋的棋盤是正方形的，棋盤的中間有一條"界河"，雙方各佔一邊。中國象棋共有32個棋子，分爲黑紅兩組，下棋的雙方各用一組。各種棋子的走法不同。兩人下棋時，紅方先走，然後輪流下棋子。當一方失去了做統帥的棋子時，另一方就贏了。當然也有不分勝負的時候，那就是和棋。1949年以後，中國象棋成爲全國正式體育比賽項目之一。

　　希望這些內容可以回答你的問題。
　　祝
工作順利！

劉明

1. Which of the following statements about Chinese chess is TRUE?

   (A) Chinese chess originated during the Song Dynasty.

   (B) Chinese chess became more popular during the Tang Dynasty.

   (C) Chinese chess and "象戏 (象戲)" are the same thing.

   (D) There are two "界河 (界河)" on the chessboard.

2. According to the rules of Chinese chess, which of the following statements is TRUE?

   (A) Each side has 32 chess pieces.

   (B) The side with the black chess pieces moves first.

   (C) All the chess pieces follow the same rules for moving.

   (D) The game may end in a draw.

Read this news.

[Simplified-character version]

中国网2005年11月9日：北京2008年奥运会吉祥物"福娃"于今日正式发布。"福娃"是五个亲密的小伙伴，每个"福娃"都有一个名字，当把五个娃娃的名字连在一起时，你会读出北京对世界的真诚邀请——"北京欢迎你"。贝贝的头部是"鱼"和"水"，它是水上运动的高手，代表奥林匹克(Olympics)五环中蓝色的环；晶晶是一只大熊猫，来自森林，代表奥林匹克五环中黑色的环；欢欢的头部是火的形状，象征奥林匹克圣火，擅长各项球类运动，代表奥林匹克五环中红色的环；迎迎是一只藏羚羊，是绿色奥运的体现，它是田径高手，代表奥林匹克五环中黄色的环；妮妮是一只燕子，其外形来自北京传统的沙燕风筝，代表奥林匹克五环中绿色的环。

[Traditional-character version]

中國網2005年11月9日：北京2008年奧運會吉祥物"福娃"於今日正式發佈。"福娃"是五個親密的小伙伴，每個"福娃"都有一個名字，當把五個娃娃的名字連在一起時，你會讀出北京對世界的真誠邀請——"北京歡迎你"。貝貝的頭部是"魚"和"水"，它是水上運動的高手，代表奧林匹克 (Olympics)五環中藍色的環；晶晶是一隻大熊貓，來自森林，代表奧林匹克五環中黑色的環；歡歡的頭部是火的形狀，象徵奧林匹克聖火，擅長各項球類運動，代表奧林匹克五環中紅色的環；迎迎是一隻藏羚羊，是綠色奧運的體現，它是田徑高手，代表奧林匹克五環中黃色的環；妮妮是一隻燕子，其外形來自北京傳統的沙燕風箏，代表奧林匹克五環中綠色的環。

3. What is the significance of the names of the five "Fu Wa"?

   (A) The names represent the five elements in Fengshui.

   (B) The names represent the five most common sports in the Olympics.

   (C) The meaning of the names represents good luck.

   (D) The pronunciation of the names means "Beijing welcomes you."

4. Which "Fu Wa" represents the features of Beijing best?

  (A) Huanhuan

  (B) Beibei

  (C) Nini

  (D) Jingjing

5. All the following "Fu Wa" are associated with an animal except _____ .

  (A) Huanhuan

  (B) Beibei

  (C) Nini

  (D) Jingjing

6. Which of the following statements about "Fu Wa" is TRUE?

  (A) Jingjing is a Tibetan antelope and represents the black ring.

  (B) Yingying is good at sports and represents the yellow ring.

  (C) Nini stands for the green ring and represents the "Green Olympics."

  (D) Huanhuan stands for the Olympic torch and represents the red ring.

Read this poster.

[Simplified-character version]	[Traditional-character version]
与名人面对面——跳水皇后归来	**與名人面對面——跳水皇后歸來**
时　　间: 2006年12月25日晚8点 地　　点: 北京体育中心 活动方式: 与高敏面对面, 听高敏讲 　　　　　自己的故事, 请高敏回答 　　　　　你的问题。	時　　間: 2006年12月25日晚8點 地　　點: 北京體育中心 活動方式: 與高敏面對面, 聽高敏講 　　　　　自己的故事, 請高敏回答 　　　　　你的問題。
高敏介绍: 　　高敏, 1986年第一次参加世界锦标赛, 就夺得女子跳水三米板的冠军。1988年, 高敏第一次获得奥运冠军。随后, 世界女子跳水开始了长达7年的"高敏时代"。在参加的所有国际比赛中, 高敏都取得了胜利。她一共获得70多块国际比赛的金牌、11项世界冠军。高敏是世界上唯一一个超过600分的女子跳水运动员, 她的技术水平和稳定性都远远超过所有对手, 是当今世界上公认的"跳水皇后"。	高敏介紹: 　　高敏, 1986年第一次參加世界錦標賽, 就奪得女子跳水三米板的冠軍。1988年, 高敏第一次獲得奧運冠軍。隨後, 世界女子跳水開始了長達7年的"高敏時代"。在參加的所有國際比賽中, 高敏都取得了勝利。她一共獲得70多塊國際比賽的金牌、11項世界冠軍。高敏是世界上唯一一個超過600分的女子跳水運動員, 她的技術水平和穩定性都遠遠超過所有對手, 是當今世界上公認的"跳水皇后"。

7. What does "与高敏面对面 (與高敏面對面)" mean here?

(A) Sit face to face with Gao Min.

(B) Interview Gao Min.

(C) Talk directly with Gao Min.

(D) Tell Gao Min your story.

8. Which of the following statements about Gao Min is TRUE?

(A) Gao Min was the world champion for swimming at the 1986 Olympic Games.

(B) Gao Min won her first international competition in 1988.

(C) Gao Min has won 70 international competitions.

(D) Gao Min has never lost an international competition.

Read this passage.

[Simplified-character version]	[Traditional-character version]
抖空竹是中国传统的体育活动,它既有娱乐性又有健身性、技术性,还具有表演性,因此一直深受老百姓的喜爱。当人们用双手抖空竹时,空竹会发出好听的声音,让人感到很愉快。空竹可以从结构、大小、功能和材料等方面进行分类。按结构可分为单头空竹（一个发声轮）和双头空竹（两个发声轮）。按功能可以分为: 练习表演空竹,即一般的练习空竹;工艺品空竹,就是既可以玩,又可以收藏的空竹;电子空竹,是指玩起来既有彩色灯光,又有音乐的那种空竹,现在它是最受年青人欢迎的。	抖空竹是中國傳統的體育活動,它既有娛樂性又有健身性、技術性,還具有表演性,因此一直深受老百姓的喜愛。當人們用雙手抖空竹時,空竹會發出好聽的聲音,讓人感到很愉快。空竹可以從結構、大小、功能和材料等方面進行分類。按結構可分爲單頭空竹（一個發聲輪）和雙頭空竹（兩個發聲輪）。按功能可分爲: 練習表演空竹,即一般的練習空竹;工藝品空竹,就是既可以玩,又可以收藏的空竹;電子空竹,是指玩起來既有彩色燈光,又有音樂的那種空竹,現在它是最受年青人歡迎的。

9. How are "工艺品空竹 (工藝品空竹)" categorized?

(A) By structure

(B) By type of material

(C) By size

(D) By function

10. According to the passage, what kind of diabolos is popular among teenagers?

(A) Double-wheel diabolos

(B) Handmade diabolos

(C) Electronic diabolos

(D) Single-wheel diabolos

Read this notice.

[Simplified-character version]	[Traditional-character version]

欢迎参加
2007年"走进中国女排"夏令营

"让中国女排认识你,让你感受中国女排,让你和中国女排一起欢笑,共同成长!"

活动时间：2007年学校暑假期间(10天)
地　　点：中国女排训练场
报名条件：初中或高中在校学生。身体健康,对排球有一定的了解,会打排球更好。
活动内容：参加中国女排的训练,与中国女排一起生活。
费　　用：每人2000元(包括午餐费、住宿费、交通费,不含早餐及晚餐费)

联系方式：
　电话：010–66668625
　传真：010–66668473
　网址：www.ine.com.cn
　邮箱：consultant@ine.com.cn
　地址：北京市海淀区新街口大街40号A栋222室
　邮编：100016

活动安排：
　第1天　星期六从公司出发,坐车到女排训练场,与女排一起吃午饭,下午参观女排训练场。晚上是欢迎晚会。
　第2天　上午请女排运动员讲自己的故事,下午与女排一起训练。
　第10天　上午与女排合影,并一起吃饭,下午坐车返回公司。

绿叶文化传播中心
2007年1月

歡迎參加
2007年"走進中國女排"夏令營

"讓中國女排認識你,讓你感受中國女排,讓你和中國女排一起歡笑,共同成長!"

活動時間：2007年學校暑假期間(10天)
地　　點：中國女排訓練場
報名條件：初中或高中在校學生。身體健康,對排球有一定的瞭解,會打排球更好。
活動內容：參加中國女排的訓練,與中國女排一起生活。
費　　用：每人2000元(包括午餐費、住宿費、交通費,不含早餐及晚餐費)

聯繫方式：
　電話：010–66668625
　傳真：010–66668473
　網址：www.ine.com.cn
　郵箱：consultant@ine.com.cn
　地址：北京市海淀區新街口大街40號A棟222室
　郵編：100016

活動安排：
　第1天　星期六從公司出發,坐車到女排訓練場,與女排一起吃午飯,下午參觀女排訓練場。晚上是歡迎晚會。
　第2天　上午請女排運動員講自己的故事,下午與女排一起訓練。
　第10天　上午與女排合影,並一起吃飯,下午坐車返回公司。

綠葉文化傳播中心
2007年1月

11. What is the purpose of this summer camp?
    (A) To teach high school students how to play volleyball.
    (B) To teach middle school students how to play volleyball.
    (C) To allow students to experience the life of the national women's volleyball team.
    (D) To allow students to visit the training center and interview the team.

12. Who can register for this activity?
    (A) Middle school students who are new to volleyball.
    (B) Primary school students who are volleyball players already.
    (C) University freshmen who are not familiar with volleyball.
    (D) High school students who have some knowledge of volleyball.

13. Which of the following statements is TRUE?
    (A) The fees include three meals a day.
    (B) The summer camp will end on a Monday.
    (C) The participants will spend their second day at a party with the national women's volleyball team.
    (D) The participants will spend their first day in training with the national women's volleyball team.

Read this passage.

[Simplified-character version]

中国人自己的体育品牌——李宁

　　李宁是世界著名的体操运动员,退役后,他于1990年成立了李宁公司。李宁牌商标是由汉语拼音"LI"和"NING"的第一个大写字母"L"和"N"构成的,以红色为主,象征着青春和热情。十几年来,李宁公司由原先生产单一运动服装的小公司发展成为拥有运动服装、运动鞋、运动器材等多项产品系列的专业化体育用品公司。随着"李宁"产品种类的日益增加,"李宁"在中国体育用品行业的地位也越来越重要。目前,"李宁"已经是中国体育用品的第一品牌。"不做中国的耐克,要做世界的李宁!"——这是李宁努力追求的目标。

[Traditional-character version]

中國人自己的體育品牌——李寧

　　李寧是世界著名的體操運動員,退役後,他於1990年成立了李寧公司。李寧牌商標是由漢語拼音"LI"和"NING"的第一個大寫字母"L"和"N"構成的,以紅色爲主,象徵著青春和熱情。十幾年來,李寧公司由原先生產單一運動服裝的小公司發展爲擁有運動服裝、運動鞋、運動器材等多項產品系列的專業化體育用品公司。隨著"李寧"產品種類的日益增加,"李寧"在中國體育用品行業的地位也越來越重要。目前,"李寧"已經是中國體育用品的第一品牌。"不做中國的耐克,要做世界的李寧!"——這是李寧努力追求的目標。

14. This passage is probably _____ .

    (A) an advertisement for Li Ning

    (B) an introduction to Li Ning

    (C) a news item about Li Ning

    (D) an introduction to Li Ning's products

15. What does "不做中国的耐克，要做世界的李宁 (不做中國的耐克，要做世界的李寧)" mean?

    (A) Li Ning is going to become a more famous brand than Nike.

    (B) Nike was a leading brand in China but Li Ning took its place.

    (C) Nike is an international brand and Li Ning is going to become one too.

    (D) Li Ning is going to take the place of Nike and become an international brand.

16. According to the passage, which of the following statements is TRUE?

    (A) Li Ning's brand logo is red.

    (B) Li Ning's brand name is the *pinyin* of "李宁 (李寧)."

    (C) Li Ning's advertising slogan is "Youth and Passion."

    (D) Li Ning started his business after he retired from competitions.

Read this note.

Simplified Character version

小宇哥：

    学校通知我们全班同学去参加北京电视台的"快乐周末"活动。这是电视台的一个娱乐性节目，要求每一个去的人至少准备一个节目，节目中可能要进行表演。节目的种类不限。我想来想去，都没有想出合适的节目。爷爷说，你的小提琴拉得很好，他建议我找你帮忙。我想请你和我一起出一个节目。要是你同意，明天晚上8点来我家吧，我们一起练习一下。对了，来时别忘记带上你的小提琴。

                      明明

                 2006–12–13

Traditional Character version

小宇哥：

    學校通知我們全班同學去參加北京電視臺的"快樂周末"活動。這是電視臺的一個娛樂性節目，要求每一個去的人至少準備一個節目，節目中可能要進行表演。節目的種類不限。我想來想去，都沒有想出合適的節目。爺爺說，你的小提琴拉得很好，他建議我找你幫忙。我想請你和我一起出一個節目。要是你同意，明天晚上8點來我家吧，我們一起練習一下。對了，來時別忘記帶上你的小提琴。

                      明明

                 2006–12–13

17. Why is Mingming looking for Xiao Yu?

   (A) Because he wants to practice the piano with him.

   (B) Because he needs help with his homework.

   (C) Because his grandfather suggested that he ask Xiao Yu for help with his performance.

   (D) Because he needs to borrow some money from him.

18. When does Xiao Yu need to go to Mingming's place?

   (A) 8:00 am, December 15

   (B) 8:00 pm, December 15

   (C) 8:00 am, December 14

   (D) 8:00 pm, December 14

Read this passage.

[Simplified-character version]	[Traditional-character version]
《女足9号》的姐妹篇——《女篮5号》是由谢晋导演的电影,它是中国第一部彩色的体育故事片,曾两次获国际奖。影片通过对林洁、林小洁母女两代人不同经历的描写,反映了不同时代体育运动员的不同命运。电影把主人公的感情变化和成长过程结合起来,很好地表现了人的感情,体现了导演独特的风格。虽然当时的电影技术不太好,但由于这是中国第一部反映中国体育的彩色电影,所以很受欢迎。近几年来,虽然电影技术很发达,却很少见到这样优秀的电影了。 ——摘自《中国电影》杂志	《女足9號》的姐妹篇——《女籃5號》是由謝晉導演的電影,它是中國第一部彩色的體育故事片,曾兩次獲國際獎。影片通過對林潔、林小潔母女兩代人不同經歷的描寫,反映了不同時代體育運動員的不同命運。電影把主人公的感情變化和成長過程結合起來,很好地表現了人的感情,體現了導演獨特的風格。雖然當時的電影技術不太好,但由於這是中國第一部反映中國體育的彩色電影,所以很受歡迎。近幾年來,雖然電影技術很發達,卻很少見到這樣優秀的電影了。 ——摘自《中國電影》雜誌

19. According to the passage, which of the following statements about the movie《女篮5号》(《女籃5號》) is TRUE?

   (A) It was released at the same time as the movie《女足9号》(《女足9號》).

   (B) It has won at least one international award.

   (C) It reflects the experiences of a mother and her daughter.

   (D) It is the first feature movie made about sports in China.

20. Which of the following statements about Xie Jin is TRUE?

(A) He has a very individual style.

(B) His movies do not usually reflect Chinese society.

(C) He mainly directs movies about sports.

(D) He is not very famous in China.

Read this advertisement.

[Simplified-character version]

招收新会员

本俱乐部以登山为主，主要在北京的郊区活动。俱乐部的宗旨是：走进自然，运动健身；享受生活，加深友情。

➤ 报名方式（任选一种）：
1. 网上报名，网址是www.dengshan.com，这是我们大力推荐的报名方式。
2. 电话，你可以拨打010—55889977报名。

➤ 费用：
每次活动收取每人10元的服务费，食宿由会员自己负责。俱乐部活动可能因为天气原因或报名人数太少（6人以下）而取消。如果活动取消，俱乐部会退回全部费用。

➤ 会员享受的服务：
1. 免费为会员举办登山运动相关知识的讲座、聚会。
2. 凭会员卡在指定商店购物时享受商品（特价商品除外）9折优惠。
3. 会员租借俱乐部装备享受8折优惠。
4. 为会员提供低于市场价格的旅游汽车出租服务。

田野户外运动俱乐部
2006-12-14

[Traditional-character version]

招收新會員

本俱樂部以登山爲主，主要在北京的郊區活動。俱樂部的宗旨是：走進自然，運動健身；享受生活，加深友情。

➤ 報名方式（任選一種）：
1. 網上報名，網址是www.dengshan.com，這是我們大力推薦的報名方式。
2. 電話，你可以撥打010—55889977報名。

➤ 費用：
每次活動收取每人10元的服務費，食宿由會員自己負責。俱樂部活動可能因爲天氣原因或報名人數太少（6人以下）而取消。如果活動取消，俱樂部會退回全部費用。

➤ 會員享受的服務：
1. 免費爲會員舉辦登山運動相關知識的講座、聚會。
2. 憑會員卡在指定商店購物時享受商品（特價商品除外）9折優惠。
3. 會員租借俱樂部裝備享受8折優惠。
4. 爲會員提供低於市場價格的旅遊汽車出租服務。

田野户外運動俱樂部
2006-12-14

21. What is the preferred mode of registration?

    (A) By phone

    (B) By post

    (C) By text message

    (D) Online

22. According to the passage, which of the following statements is TRUE?

    (A) Food and lodging are always included.

    (B) If an activity is canceled, members will receive a partial refund.

    (C) Members get a 10% discount on all purchases at certain stores.

    (D) Members can attend some lectures and events for free.

Read this letter.

[Simplified-character version]	[Traditional-character version]
张老师: 　　您好! 　　您最近身体好吗? 我这里一切还好, 只是觉得大学课程比较难, 学习安排有些紧张。 　　最近我看了一场杂技表演, 就是我在高中时您告诉过我的那个杂技团。报纸上说它是中国最有名的杂技团。那天他们表演了很多节目, 看起来都很危险。看的时候我非常紧张, 可是那些表演的人看上去却很轻松。有个小女孩表演的时候差点儿从钢丝上掉下来, 不过她的表演还是很精彩的。演出后我看了一些资料, 才知道杂技在很早以前就有了, 而且, 因为杂技里很多项目都和劳动技术有关, 所以一些人认为杂技是从劳动发展而来的。 …… 　　　　　　　　　　娜娜 　　　　　　　　2006-12-14	張老師: 　　您好! 　　您最近身體好嗎? 我這裏一切還好, 只是覺得大學課程比較難, 學習安排有些緊張。 　　最近我看了一場雜技表演, 就是我在高中時您告訴過我的那個雜技團。報紙上說它是中國最有名的雜技團。那天他們表演了很多節目, 看起來都很危險。看的時候我非常緊張, 可是那些表演的人看上去卻很輕鬆。有個小女孩表演的時候差點兒從鋼絲上掉下來, 不過她的表演還是很精彩的。演出後我看了一些資料, 才知道雜技在很早以前就有了, 而且, 因爲雜技裏很多項目都和勞動技術有關, 所以一些人認爲雜技是從勞動發展而來的。 …… 　　　　　　　　　　娜娜 　　　　　　　　2006-12-14

23. 张老师 (張老師) is probably Nana's _____ .

    (A) senior high school teacher

    (B) university lecturer

    (C) private tutor

    (D) acrobatics instructor

24. What happened during the acrobatics performance?

(A) Nana refused to perform.

(B) The audience cheered too loudly and distracted the performers.

(C) A female performer almost fell down.

(D) The lights went out.

Read this phrase.

[Simplified-character version]   [Traditional-character version]

内有照片，勿折   内有照片，勿摺

25. Where would this sign most likely appear?

(A) On a poster

(B) On an envelope

(C) In a purse

(D) On a photo

26. What is the purpose of this phrase?

(A) To indicate the importance of an item.

(B) To indicate that photos should not be photocopied.

(C) To tell others not to fold this item.

(D) To show that this item is private.

Read this public sign.

[Simplified-character version]   [Traditional-character version]

生命在于运动   生命在於運動

27. Where would this sign most likely appear?

(A) In a library

(B) In a cinema

(C) In a sports club

(D) In a department store

28. Which of the following statements about this sign is TRUE?

(A) It says that it is important to eat healthily.

(B) It says that everyone should join a sports club.

(C) It says that it is important to exercise.

(D) It says that people should pursue a healthy lifestyle.

Section Two

I. Free Response (Writing)

Note: In this part, you may NOT move back and forth among questions.

Directions: You will be asked to write in Chinese in a variety of ways. In each case, you will be asked to write for a specific purpose and to a specific person. You should write in as complete and as culturally appropriate a manner as possible, taking into account the purpose and the person described.

1. Story Narration

The four pictures present a story. Imagine you are writing the story to a friend. Narrate a complete story as suggested by the pictures. Give your story a beginning, a middle, and an end.

2. Personal Letter

Imagine you received a letter from a pen pal. The letter talks about your pen pal's ideas about a healthy lifestyle and their intention to discuss this topic with you. Write a reply in letter format. Write about your opinion on healthy living. Tell your pen pal if you agree or disagree with their ideas. Justify your opinion with specific examples.

3. E-Mail Response

Read this e-mail from a friend and then type a response.

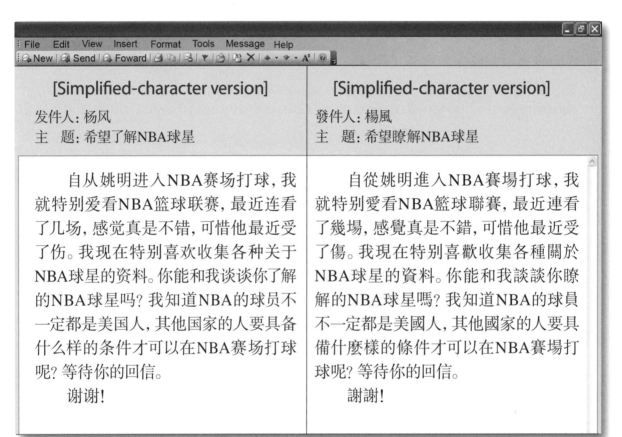

| File | Edit | View | Insert | Format | Tools | Message | Help |

New | Send | Foward

[Simplified-character version]	[Simplified-character version]
发件人: 杨风	發件人: 楊風
主 题: 希望了解NBA球星	主 题: 希望瞭解NBA球星
自从姚明进入NBA赛场打球, 我就特别爱看NBA篮球联赛, 最近连看了几场, 感觉真是不错, 可惜他最近受了伤。我现在特别喜欢收集各种关于NBA球星的资料。你能和我谈谈你了解的NBA球星吗? 我知道NBA的球员不一定都是美国人, 其他国家的人要具备什么样的条件才可以在NBA赛场打球呢? 等待你的回信。	自從姚明進入NBA賽場打球, 我就特別愛看NBA籃球聯賽, 最近連看了幾場, 感覺真是不錯, 可惜他最近受了傷。我現在特別喜歡收集各種關於NBA球星的資料。你能和我談談你瞭解的NBA球星嗎? 我知道NBA的球員不一定都是美國人, 其他國家的人要具備什麼樣的條件才可以在NBA賽場打球呢? 等待你的回信。
谢谢!	謝謝!

4. Relay a Telephone Message

Imagine you are sharing an apartment with some Chinese friends. You arrive home one day and listen to a message on the answering machine. The message is for one of those friends. You will listen twice to the message. Then relay the message, including the important details, by typing an e-mail to your friend.

II. Free Response (Speaking)

Note: In this part, you may NOT move back and forth among questions.

Directions: You will participate in a simulated conversation. Each time it is your turn to speak, you will have 20 seconds to record. You should respond as fully and as appropriately as possible.

1. Conversation

You are chatting with your friend, a senior high school student in China about sports activities.

Directions: You will be asked to speak in Chinese on context topics in the following two questions. In each case, imagine you are making an oral presentation to your Chinese class. First, you will read and hear the topic for your presentation. You will have 4 minutes to prepare your presentation. Then you will have 2 minutes to record your presentation. Your presentation should be as complete as possible.

2. Cultural Presentation

There are many different schools of Chinese martial arts. Choose ONE, Such as *Taiji*, and talk about it in as much detail as you can.

3. Event Plan

You have the opportunity to organize a class activity outdoors, such as trekking or mountain climbing. In your presentation, describe the advantages and disadvantages of different options. Also explain what you would prepare for the activity and other matters that require attention.

UNIT ONE
LESSON 2
Sports and Fitness
What's Your Favorite Sport?

Section One

I. Multiple Choice (Listen to the dialogs)

Note: In this part, you may NOT move back and forth among questions.

Directions: In this part, you will hear several short conversations or parts of conversations followed by four choices, designated (A), (B), (C), and (D). Choose the one that continues or completes the conversation in a logical and culturally appropriate manner. You will have 5 seconds to answer each question.

1.	(A)	(B)	(C)	(D)	5.	(A)	(B)	(C)	(D)
2.	(A)	(B)	(C)	(D)	6.	(A)	(B)	(C)	(D)
3.	(A)	(B)	(C)	(D)	7.	(A)	(B)	(C)	(D)
4.	(A)	(B)	(C)	(D)	8.	(A)	(B)	(C)	(D)

II. Multiple Choice (Listen to the selections)

Note: In this part, you may move back and forth only among the questions associated with the current listening selection.

Directions: In this part, you will listen to several selections in Chinese. For each selection, you will be told whether it will be played once or twice. You may take notes as you listen. After listening to each selection, you will see questions in English. For each question, choose the response that is best according to the selection. You will have 12 seconds to answer each question.

Selection 1

1. The recording is most likely _____ .
   (A) a radio broadcast
   (B) an audio clip taken from a movie
   (C) a TV broadcast
   (D) an advertisement

2. What is the score in the second game of the match?
   (A) China is leading by 11 points to 9.
   (B) Korea is leading by 11 points to 9.
   (C) China is leading by 11 points to 8.
   (D) Korea is leading by 11 points to 8.

3. What is the final result?
   (A) Korea won.
   (B) China won.
   (C) The game ended in a draw.
   (D) The game is not over yet.

Selection 2

4. Where does Zhang Hua invite Xiao Li to go?
   (A) The swimming pool
   (B) The badminton court
   (C) The basketball court
   (D) The sports center

5. Why does Zhang Hua recommend this place to Xiao Li?
   (A) Because he was told that it is well-equipped and reasonably priced.
   (B) Because he likes to play badminton.
   (C) Because he saw an attractive advertisement.
   (D) Because he likes to play tennis.

6. Why is this place attractive to Zhang Hua and Xiao Li?
   (A) There is a 20% discount.
   (B) Admission is free.
   (C) There are special promotions for students.
   (D) There is a 30% discount.

Selection 3

7. How many students at this school won the first prize?
   (A) 12
   (B) 4
   (C) 9
   (D) 3

8. The students at this school did NOT win first prize in _____ .
   (A) the 1500m running event
   (B) the table tennis match
   (C) the badminton match
   (D) the swimming event

Selection 4

9. The sports center wants to hire _____ .
   (A) part-time personal trainers
   (B) part-time administrative staff
   (C) part-time swimming coaches
   (D) part-time yoga teachers

10. When is the deadline for applying for the job?
    (A) This Friday
    (B) The fifth of this month
    (C) The fifteenth of this month
    (D) This weekend

11. Where should the applicants go to apply for the job?
    (A) Room 1002 on the first floor
    (B) Room 1001 on the second floor
    (C) Room 1002 on the fifteenth floor
    (D) Room 1001 on the eleventh floor

Selection 5

12. When does the boy suggest they go mountain climbing?
    (A) The following holiday
    (B) This weekend
    (C) Saturday evening
    (D) In the morning

13. Does the girl like to go mountain climbing?
    (A) No, she thinks it's tiring.
    (B) No, she prefers to watch a movie.
    (C) Yes, but she thinks it's tiring.
    (D) Yes, but she prefers to go on another day.

14. What answer does the girl give the boy in the end?

(A) She refuses to go with him.

(B) She agrees to go with him.

(C) She tells him she will let him know tomorrow.

(D) She asks if she can bring her sister as well.

III. Multiple Choice (Reading)

Note: In this part of the exam, you may move back and forth among all the questions.

Directions: You will read several selections in Chinese. Each selection is accompanied by a number of questions in English. For each question, choose the response that is best according to the selection.

Read this letter.

[Simplified-character version]

小玲:

你好!

最近过得怎么样?还老感冒吗?冬天快到了,天气变化大,你一定要注意身体。我在学校挺好的,只是前一段时间生病了。病好以后,我每天都坚持锻炼身体,现在感觉越来越好,不像以前那样吃不下饭了,白天也挺有精神的,晚上不仅睡得着了,而且还睡得特别香。现在,我每天晚上都去学校的操场跑步。通过跑步,我的身体棒多了,也瘦了不少,真是一举两得。我建议你也每天坚持跑步,它会让你变得更健康的。

……

小明
5月7日

[Traditional-character version]

小玲:

你好!

最近過得怎麼樣?還老感冒嗎?冬天快到了,天氣變化大,你一定要注意身體。我在學校挺好的,只是前一段時間生病了。病好以後,我每天都堅持鍛煉身體,現在感覺越來越好,不像以前那樣吃不下飯了,白天也挺有精神的,晚上不僅睡得著了,而且還睡得特別香。現在,我每天晚上都去學校的操場跑步。通過跑步,我的身體棒多了,也瘦了不少,真是一舉兩得。我建議你也每天堅持跑步,它會讓你變得更健康的。

……

小明
5月7日

1. We can infer from the letter that Xiao Ming hopes Xiao Ling _____ .
    (A) will lose weight
    (B) will recover from her cold soon
    (C) will become healthier
    (D) will start eating again soon

2. According to the letter which of the following is TRUE?
    (A) Xiao Ming started to go jogging before recovering from his cold.
    (B) Xiao Ling thinks that jogging has more advantages than disadvantages.
    (C) Jogging helped Xiao Ling recover from his cold.
    (D) Xiao Ming is much slimmer than before.

Read this passage.

[Simplified-character version]	[Traditional-character version]
有人说，一个人不应该只改正他的缺点，更多地是应该发挥他的优点，我想这句话对刘若英来说是最适合不过了。虽然她现在是中国最有名的女明星之一，但是她的成名并不像大家想象的那样轻松。她以前当过家庭钢琴教师，虽然她的钢琴弹得很好，但家长对她的教学评价却非常低。她并没有因为这件事而灰心，相反地，她尝试了很多工作，最后终于找到了自己擅长和感兴趣的工作，那就是唱歌。在生活中，大家都会遇到很多在别人看来容易而自己却做不好的事情，不要紧，每个人都有自己的缺点和优点，最重要的是善于发现并充分发挥你的优点。	有人説，一個人不應該只改正他的缺點，更多地是應該發揮他的優點，我想這句話對劉若英來説是最適合不過了。雖然她現在是中國最有名的女明星之一，但是她的成名並不像大家想像的那樣輕鬆。她以前當過家庭鋼琴教師，雖然她的鋼琴彈得很好，但家長對她的教學評價卻非常低。她並沒有因爲這件事而灰心，相反地，她嘗試了很多工作，最後終於找到了自己擅長和感興趣的工作，那就是唱歌。在生活中，大家都會遇到很多在別人看來容易而自己卻做不好的事情，不要緊，每個人都有自己的缺點和優點，最重要的是善於發現並充分發揮你的優點。

3. This passage is about _____ .
    (A) how Liu Ruoying became a movie star
    (B) how everybody has their own weaknesses
    (C) how Liu Ruoying discovered her passion in singing
    (D) how everybody should make full use of their talents

4. Which of the following statements is TRUE?
    (A) Liu Ruoying was good at teaching piano.
    (B) Liu Ruoying used to change jobs quite often.
    (C) Liu Ruoying became a star overnight.
    (D) Liu Ruoying used to be one of the most famous female stars in China.

5. Which of the following pieces of advice might we derive from the passage?

    (A) When you encounter difficulties, you should not give up, but work even harder.

    (B) You should know what you are good at and make the most of it.

    (C) You should always make time to relax.

    (D) If you are going wrong, you should find the reason why immediately.

Read this notice.

[Simplified-character version]	[Traditional-character version]
第20届田径运动会的通知	**第20届田径運動會的通知**
各位同学:	各位同學:
根据2006年学校体育工作计划的安排, 我校将在2006年10月5日至6日举行第20届校运动会, 现将具体安排通知如下:	根據2006年學校體育工作計劃的安排, 我校將在2006年10月5日至6日舉行第20届校運動會, 現將具體安排通知如下:
1. 10月5日早上8时: 在西操场举行开幕式, 请各班班长组织同学在西操场看台上观看, 所有运动员请在西操场东集合。	1. 10月5日早上8時: 在西操場舉行開幕式, 请各班班長組織同學在西操場看臺上觀看, 所有運動員請在西操場東集合。
2. 10月5日9点至10月6日下午4时30分: 正式比赛, 比赛地点在学校东操场。	2. 10月5日9點至10月6日下午4時30分: 正式比賽, 比賽地點在學校東操場。
3. 10月6日下午4时30分: 在体育馆举行闭幕式, 请各位运动员准时参加。	3. 10月6日下午4時30分: 在體育館舉行閉幕式, 请各位運動員準時參加。
本次比赛和去年一样仍采取网上报名, 报名程序请点击http://www.sanshizhongxue.edu/sports。另外, 男生和女生分开报名, 高中部和初中部分为两组报名和比赛, 各组内不再分年龄组。	本次比賽和去年一樣仍採取網上報名, 報名程序請點擊http://www.sanshizhongxue.edu/sports。另外, 男生和女生分開報名, 高中部和初中部分爲兩組報名和比賽, 各組內不再分年齡組。
报名截止时间是2006年10月4日中午12时。	報名截止時間是2006年10月4日中午12時。
欢迎各位同学踊跃报名!	歡迎各位同學踴躍報名!
三市中学 2006年9月15日	三市中學 2006年9月15日

6. We know from the notice that the opening ceremony of the sports meet _____ .

(A) will be held on the eastern sports ground

(B) can be seen from the west side of the eastern sports ground

(C) will be held in the gym

(D) can be seen from the grandstand in the western sports ground

7. Which of the following statements about the application process is TRUE?

(A) It can be completed on the Internet.

(B) It is different from last year's process.

(C) It can be sent by post.

(D) It must be submitted before midnight on October 4.

8. Which of the following statements regarding the sports event is TRUE?

(A) The competition will run from 8:00 am till 4:30 pm for two days.

(B) The venue for all events is the eastern sports ground.

(C) All events are categorized by age.

(D) Students in different grades will not compete with each other.

Read this information.

Simplified-character version

新同学, 欢迎你的到来!

你打算如何度过这四年的大学生活呢? 除了从书本上学习知识, 你还可以参加学校的课外活动, 培养自己各方面的能力。校学生会为各位提供了很好的机会, 你们可以根据自己的兴趣和特长选择各种社团, 如书法、体育、绘画、音乐等。各社团一般在周末开展活动, 想报名的同学请带上学生证到校学生会报名。

报名时间 : 9月12日—9月19日, 每天中午12:00—下午1:30

报名地点 : 2号楼202室

校学生会
2006年9月7日

Traditional-character version

新同學, 歡迎你的到來!

你打算如何度過這四年的大學生活呢? 除了從書本上學習知識, 你還可以參加學校的課外活動, 培養自己各方面的能力。校學生會爲各位提供了很好的機會, 你們可以根據自己的興趣和特長選擇各種社團, 如書法、體育、繪畫、音樂等。各社團一般在週末開展活動, 想報名的同學請帶上學生證到校學生會報名。

報名時間 : 9月12日—9月19日, 每天中午12:00—下午1:30

報名地點 : 2號樓202室

校學生會
2006年9月7日

9. This information describes _____ .

    (A) how to enroll at the school

    (B) what kind of activities club members can do

    (C) what the meeting schedule for the students' association is

    (D) how to enrol at the students' clubs

10. The information is for _____ .

    (A) freshmen

    (B) sophomores

    (C) juniors

    (D) seniors

11. What can we infer from this information?

    (A) Only students who are free on weekends can join the clubs.

    (B) The enrolment period lasts for 8 days.

    (C) Students can apply for a maximum of three clubs.

    (D) Students need to pay a 5-*yuan* administration fee.

Read this passage.

[Simplified-character version]	[Traditional-character version]
北京时间2006年9月9日，中国的刘翔在德国第4届世界田径总决赛上以12秒93的好成绩在男子110米栏决赛中夺得了冠军。这是本项赛事上中国人赢得的第一个冠军。这也是他在2004年奥运会夺得金牌和今年瑞士洛桑大奖赛创造12秒88的好成绩以后，跑出的最好成绩。但就像洛桑大奖赛一样，刘翔的这个成绩连他自己也没想到，特别是今年年初他因脚伤很多比赛都没有参加，因而这次的成绩让所有的人都非常惊讶。记者认为，刘翔的技术是他获得好成绩的基础，但能跑出12秒88和12秒93的成绩，也是因为他的心态好。同样，在下个月的上海大奖赛中，刘翔的心态如何将成为他能否夺取金牌的关键，12秒93的成绩可能会对他有些影响。	北京時間2006年9月9日，中國的劉翔在德國第4屆世界田徑總決賽上以12秒93的好成績在男子110米欄決賽中奪得了冠軍。這是本項賽事上中國人贏得的第一個冠軍。這也是他在2004年奧運會奪得金牌和今年瑞士洛桑大獎賽創造12秒88的好成績以後，跑出的最好成績。但就像洛桑大獎賽一樣，劉翔的這個成績連他自己也沒想到，特別是今年年初他因腳傷很多比賽都沒有參加，因而這次的成績讓所有的人都非常驚訝。記者認爲，劉翔的技術是他獲得好成績的基礎，但能跑出12秒88和12秒93的成績，也是因爲他的心態好。同樣，在下個月的上海大獎賽中，劉翔的心態如何將成爲他能否奪取金牌的關鍵，12秒93的成績可能會對他有些影響。

12. This passage is probably _____ .

   (A) an advertisement

   (B) a speech

   (C) a news commentary

   (D) a government announcement

13. According to the passage, which of the following statements is TRUE?

   (A) Liu Xiang had a serious injury so he couldn't compete in competitions for eight months.

   (B) Liu Xiang set a world record for the 110m hurdles in Germany.

   (C) Liu Xiang was confident that he would win the competition in Germany.

   (D) Liu Xiang's fastest time in the 110m hurdles is 12.88 seconds.

14. According to the passage, what will affect Liu Xiang's performance in his next competition?

   (A) Whether his injuries can fully heal.

   (B) Whether he has enough time to rest.

   (C) Whether the results he set previously put too much pressure on him.

   (D) Whether he is able to maintain his fitness.

Read this information.

[Simplified-character version]

同学们：
　　大家以前都玩过乒乓球，但据我了解，大多数同学都是第一次参加乒乓球比赛，下面我具体讲一下比赛的规则。
　　首先，一场乒乓球比赛通常包括五局或三局。在五局中，先胜三局的一方获胜；在三局中，先胜两局的一方为胜方，但得分必须超过对方2分。一场比赛将连续进行，但在局与局之间，任何一名运动员都有权要求不超过两分钟的休息时间。
　　第二是关于发球规则。发球方发了两个球以后，交换发球，接球方将成为发球方。双方比分如果都达到10分，发球和接球顺序不变，但此后每人只发一个球。一局中首先发球的一方，在下一局中应首先接球。
　　大家都清楚了吗？

[Traditional-character version]

同學們：
　　大家以前都玩過乒乓球，但據我瞭解，大多數同學都是第一次參加乒乓球比賽，下面我具體講一下比賽的規則。
　　首先，一場乒乓球比賽通常包括五局或三局。在五局中，先勝三局的一方獲勝；在三局中，先勝兩局的一方獲勝。在每局比賽中，每一個選手打贏一個球得1分，先得11分的一方爲勝方，但得分必須超過對方2分。一場比賽將連續進行，但在局與局之間，任何一名運動員都有權要求不超過兩分鐘的休息時間。
　　第二是關於發球規則。發球方發了兩個球以後，交換發球，接球方將成爲發球方。雙方比分如果都達到10分，發球和接球順序不變，但此後每人只發一個球。一局中首先發球的一方，在下一局中應首先接球。
　　大家都清楚了嗎？

15. If the score is 11:10 in a set, then _____ .

    (A) the player with 11 points wins

    (B) nobody has won yet

    (C) the players may rest for 2 minutes

    (D) the players play another set

16. When the score is 10:10, the player who just served will _____ .

    (A) serve one more time

    (B) receive the next serve

    (C) serve two more times

    (D) receive the next two serves

Read this passage.

[Simplified-character version]

自古以来，中国的武术就有踢、打、摔、拿、跌五种不同的练习方法，太极拳的练习方法就是以打为主。太极拳的练习方法要求先慢后快，再由快变慢。慢要慢到别人跟不上，快要快到出乎别人的意料。练习的时候要用四肢打出弧形的动作，但不需要用太大的力气，同时要求身体端正，全身放松，注意力集中，尽量作深呼吸。这种将四肢动作、意识和呼吸相结合的练习方法对人们锻炼身体、修身养性有很大的好处。

[Traditional-character version]

自古以來，中國的武術就有踢、打、摔、拿、跌五種不同的練習方法，太極拳的練習方法就是以打爲主。太極拳的練習方法要求先慢後快，再由快變慢。慢要慢到別人跟不上，快要快到出乎別人的意料。練習的時候要用四肢打出弧形的動作，但不需要用太大的力氣，同時要求身體端正，全身放鬆，注意力集中，儘量作深呼吸。這種將四肢動作、意識和呼吸相結合的練習方法對人們鍛煉身體、修身養性有很大的好處。

17. What is the passage about?

    (A) The different schools of Chinese martial arts.

    (B) The popularity of *Taiji* around the world.

    (C) The way *Taiji* should be practiced.

    (D) The reason Chinese people like *Taiji*.

18. According to the passage, when practicing *Taiji*, you should _____ .

(A) move at the same speed at all times

(B) keep every movement slow

(C) closely follow the movements of your instructor

(D) vary the speed of your movements

Read this passage.

[Simplified-character version]

11月5日　　晴

　　今天下午孩子问了我一个问题，他想知道我小时候都玩些什么。我一时没答上来。那时没有玩具，家里既没有电视，也没有网络，我们到底玩什么呢？儿子的这个问题让我想起了自己小时候的生活。那时，我经常和邻居家的小伙伴们一起去游泳，爬树。我也非常喜欢植物，常常从附近的小山上移来一些野花，将它们种在我们家的房屋旁。二十年过去了，附近的小山上已盖了一家工厂，房屋旁也找不着空地了，看到的只是一栋栋的高楼。虽然现在的孩子们玩的东西多了，但是他们离大自然却越来越远了。

[Traditional-character version]

11月5日　　晴

　　今天下午孩子問了我一個問題，他想知道我小時候都玩些什麼。我一時沒答上來。那時沒有玩具，家裏既沒有電視，也沒有網絡，我們到底玩什麼呢？兒子的這個問題讓我想起了自己小時候的生活。那時，我經常和鄰居家的小伙伴們一起去游泳，爬樹。我也非常喜歡植物，常常從附近的小山上移來一些野花，將它們種在我們家的房屋旁。二十年過去了，附近的小山上已蓋了一家工廠，房屋旁也找不著空地了，看到的只是一棟棟的高樓。雖然現在的孩子們玩的東西多了，但是他們離大自然卻越來越遠了。

19. This passage is probably taken from _____ .

(A) an e-mail

(B) an editorial

(C) a diary entry

(D) a letter

20. Which of the following statements is TRUE?

(A) The author used to watch TV quite often as a child.

(B) The author used to play at their neighbor's house as a child.

(C) The author used to read a lot of books as a child.

(D) The author used to play with their friends a lot as a child.

21. We can infer from this passage that the author thinks children nowadays _____.

    (A) have few things to play with

    (B) don't have a chance to enjoy nature

    (C) exercise very little

    (D) do not have enough friends

Read this public sign.

[Simplified-character version]   [Traditional-character version]

凭票入场   憑票入場

22. Where would this sign most likely appear?

    (A) At a customer service counter

    (B) In a restaurant

    (C) In a cinema

    (D) At a bus station

23. What does this sign mean?

    (A) This is the place you buy tickets.

    (B) You should hold on your ticket at all times.

    (C) You can buy tickets at the counter.

    (D) You cannot enter without a ticket.

Read this public sign.

[Simplified-character version]   [Traditional-character version]

小心地滑   小心地滑

24. Where would this sign most likely appear?

    (A) At a sports ground

    (B) In a classroom

    (C) In a public toilet

    (D) At a skating rink

25. What does this sign mean?

    (A) Skate carefully.

    (B) Skate slowly.

    (C) Be aware of ice on the ground.

    (D) Be careful not to slip and fall.

Section Two

I. Free Response (Writing)

Note: In this part, you may NOT move back and forth among questions.

Directions: You will be asked to write in Chinese in a variety of ways. In each case, you will be asked to write for a specific purpose and to a specific person. You should write in as complete and as culturally appropriate a manner as possible, taking into account the purpose and the person described.

1. Story Narration

The four pictures present a story. Imagine you are writing the story to a friend. Narrate a complete story as suggested by the pictures. Give your story a beginning, a middle, and an end.

2. Personal Letter

Imagine you received a letter from a pen pal. He mentions that he likes "strength sports" (weightlifting, body building, etc.) very much and would like to discuss this topic with you. Write a reply in letter format. First, write about what kind of "strength sports" are common in high schools in the United States. Then explain why you like or dislike these sports. Justify your opinion with specific examples.

3. E-Mail Response

Read this e-mail from a friend and then type a response.

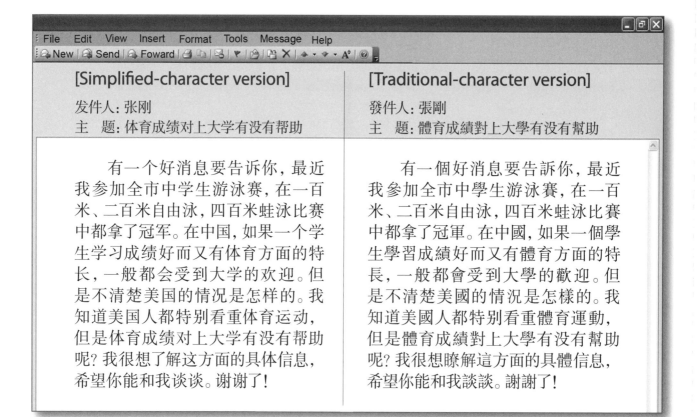

File　Edit　View　Insert　Format　Tools　Message　Help

New | Send | Foward | | | | | | X | | | | A |

[Simplified-character version]

发件人: 张刚
主　题: 体育成绩对上大学有没有帮助

　　有一个好消息要告诉你，最近我参加全市中学生游泳赛，在一百米、二百米自由泳，四百米蛙泳比赛中都拿了冠军。在中国，如果一个学生学习成绩好而又有体育方面的特长，一般都会受到大学的欢迎。但是不清楚美国的情况是怎样的。我知道美国人都特别看重体育运动，但是体育成绩对上大学有没有帮助呢? 我很想了解这方面的具体信息，希望你能和我谈谈。谢谢了!

[Traditional-character version]

發件人: 張剛
主　題: 體育成績對上大學有沒有幫助

　　有一個好消息要告訴你，最近我參加全市中學生游泳賽，在一百米、二百米自由泳，四百米蛙泳比賽中都拿了冠軍。在中國，如果一個學生學習成績好而又有體育方面的特長，一般都會受到大學的歡迎。但是不清楚美國的情況是怎樣的。我知道美國人都特別看重體育運動，但是體育成績對上大學有沒有幫助呢? 我很想瞭解這方面的具體信息，希望你能和我談談。謝謝了!

4. Relay a Telephone Message

Imagine you are a high school student called Qiangqiang. You arrive home one day and listen to a message on the answering machine. The message is from your mother. She wants you to pass a message to your father. However, you are about to go out to your friend's party. You will listen twice to the message. Then relay the message, including the important details, by typing a note to your father.

II. Free Response (Speaking)

Note: In this part, you may NOT move back and forth among questions.

Directions: You will participate in a simulated conversation. Each time it is your turn to speak, you will have 20 seconds to record. You should respond as fully and as appropriately as possible.

1. Conversation

You will have a conversation with Huang Hua, a school news reporter, about your views on the variety of subjects being offered at your school.

Directions: You will be asked to speak in Chinese on different topics in the following two questions. In each case, imagine you are making an oral presentation to your class in Chinese. First, you will read and hear the topic of your presentation. You will have 4 minutes to prepare your presentation. Then you will have 2 minutes to record your presentation. Your presentation should be as complete as possible.

2. Cultural Presentation

Choose ONE traditional Chinese sport you know (kite flying, dragon boat racing, etc.). In your presentation, describe your understanding of this sport in as much detail as possible.

3. Event Plan

You have the opportunity to organize a basketball game with another class of the same grade. In your presentation, explain your plan to your classmates (how to prepare, matters that require attention, etc.), reasons for organizing this game, and persuade them to accept your plan and to participate in the game.

UNIT TWO
LESSON 3
Food and Fashion
The Beijing Teahouse

Section One

I. Multiple Choice (Listen to the dialogs)

Note: In this part, you may NOT move back and forth among questions.

Directions: In this part, you will hear several short conversations or parts of conversations followed by four choices, designated (A), (B), (C), and (D). Choose the one that continues or completes the conversation in a logical and culturally appropriate manner. You will have 5 seconds to answer each question.

1.	(A)	(B)	(C)	(D)	5.	(A)	(B)	(C)	(D)
2.	(A)	(B)	(C)	(D)	6.	(A)	(B)	(C)	(D)
3.	(A)	(B)	(C)	(D)	7.	(A)	(B)	(C)	(D)
4.	(A)	(B)	(C)	(D)	8.	(A)	(B)	(C)	(D)

II. Multiple Choice (Listen to the selections)

Note: In this part, you may move back and forth only among the questions associated with the current listening selection.

Directions: In this part, you will listen to several selections in Chinese. For each selection, you will be told whether it will be played once or twice. You may take notes as you listen. After listening to each selection, you will see questions in English. For each question, choose the response that is best according to the selection. You will have 12 seconds to answer each question.

Selection 1

1. When will the students go to the Laoshe Teahouse?
   - (A) In the morning
   - (B) In the afternoon
   - (C) In the evening
   - (D) At noon

2. How did the Laoshe Teahouse get its name?
(A) It was named after a famous play.
(B) It was named after a historical place.
(C) It was named after the owner's teacher.
(D) It was named after a well-known historian.

3. What is special about the Laoshe Teahouse?
(A) It has a very long history.
(B) It features Beijing opera performances.
(C) It has a very unusual location.
(D) It has a very broad selection of teas.

Selection 2

4. Where do the students usually meet?
(A) At a cafe
(B) At a teahouse
(C) At a restaurant
(D) At the school gate

5. Why doesn't the man want to go to the place the woman suggests?
(A) Because it is too far away.
(B) Because he doesn't like it.
(C) Because he heard that the drinks there are very expensive.
(D) Because he prefers the teahouse.

6. Who will probably pay tonight?
(A) The man.
(B) The woman.
(C) They will split the bill.
(D) No one; the man knows the owner.

Selection 3

7. When did Li Qiang call?
(A) In the morning
(B) At noon
(C) In the afternoon
(D) In the evening

8. Why does Li Qiang want to invite Wang Jian to dinner?
   (A) Because they haven't seen each other for a long time.
   (B) Because they often eat dinner together.
   (C) Because his younger sister wants to get to know Wang Jian.
   (D) Because he knows that Wang Jian likes eating braised goose.

9. Where will they have dinner tomorrow?
   (A) At a fast food restaurant.
   (B) At a cafe.
   (C) At a braised goose restaurant on Anding Men Street.
   (D) Anywhere Wang Jian wants.

Selection 4

10. How many of them will eat at the restaurant?
    (A) Five
    (B) Three
    (C) Seven
    (D) Four

11. What type of food is served in this restaurant?
    (A) Beijing food
    (B) Sichuan food
    (C) Hunan food
    (D) Xinjiang food

12. Which of the following statements about the guests is TRUE?
    (A) They often come to this restaurant to eat.
    (B) They cannot eat spicy food.
    (C) They want to sit by the window.
    (D) They want their food served right now.

Selection 5

13. When did Mr. Wang call the restaurant?
    (A) January 2
    (B) January 18
    (C) January 20
    (D) January 22

14. Why did Mr. Wang call the restaurant?

   (A) To reserve a table for dinner.

   (B) To reserve a private room.

   (C) To ask about the chef.

   (D) To order some dishes in advance.

15. Which of the following statements is TRUE?

   (A) Mr. Wang reserved a room for four people.

   (B) Mr. Wang left his telephone number.

   (C) Mr. Wang left his full name.

   (D) Mr. Wang has to call the restaurant again.

III. Multiple Choice (Reading)

Note: In this part, you may move back and forth among all the questions.

Directions: You will read several selections in Chinese. Each selection is accompanied by a number of questions in English. For each question, choose the response that is best according to the selection.

Read this passage.

[Simplified-character version]	[Traditional-character version]
我刚到中国北方的时候觉得很不适应。在南方, 我们的主食是米饭, 可来到北方以后, 北方人习惯吃面食, 如面条、饼、饺子什么的, 这些都是他们一日三餐的主食, 对于习惯吃米饭的我来说, 真不能接受。我想南北方主食的不同主要是因为南北方有不同的气候: 南方雨水充足、湿润, 适合水稻的生长, 因而以米饭为主; 北方很少下雨, 干燥, 更适合小麦的生长, 因而以面食为主。	我剛到中國北方的時候覺得很不適應。在南方, 我們的主食是米飯, 可來到北方以後, 北方人習慣吃麵食, 如麵條、餅、餃子什麼的, 這些都是他們一日三餐的主食, 對於習慣吃米飯的我來說, 真不能接受。我想南北方主食的不同主要是因爲南北方有不同的氣候: 南方雨水充足、濕潤, 適合水稻的生長, 因而以米飯爲主; 北方很少下雨, 乾燥, 更適合小麥的生長, 因而以麵食爲主。

1. According to the passage, why couldn't the author get used to northern China?
   (A) Because it rains a lot in the south but rarely rains in the north.
   (B) Because it is hot in the south but cold in the north.
   (C) Because staple foods in the south are different from those in the north.
   (D) Because he likes foods that are difficult to get in the north.

2. Which of the following statements is TRUE?
   (A) Rice grows in dry places.
   (B) Wheat grows in wet places.
   (C) Southern China is rich in rice.
   (D) Southern China is rich in wheat.

Read this letter.

[Simplified-character version]

杰克:
　　你好!
　　我现在在中国过得很好,吃住都很适应。来中国以前,我很少去中餐厅,一来我家附近就只有一家中餐厅,菜肴的种类不是很多,味道也很一般,二来在饭店里吃饭太贵了,不可能经常去吃。现在来中国了,我发现这里的中餐跟美国的中餐很不一样,不但种类很多,味道可口,更重要的是中国菜非常便宜,比起国内的中国菜来真算得上是物美价廉。我现在每餐都吃中国菜,但是也去吃过西餐。这里的西餐,口味、种类也和美国的有很大的不同,和美国的中餐一样不地道。我想我以后不会再去这里的饭店吃西餐了。
　　……
罗丝
3月1日

[Traditional-character version]

傑克:
　　你好!
　　我現在在中國過得很好,吃住都很適應。來中國以前,我很少去中餐廳,一來我家附近就只有一家中餐廳,菜餚的種類也不是很多,味道也很一般,二來在飯店裏吃飯太貴了,不可能經常去吃。現在來中國了,我發現這裏的中餐跟美國的中餐很不一樣,不但種類很多,味道可口,更重要的是中國菜非常便宜,比起國內的中國菜來真算得上是物美價廉。我現在每餐都吃中國菜,但是也去吃過西餐。這裏的西餐,口味、種類也和美國的有很大的不同,和美國的中餐一樣不地道。我想我以後不會再去這裏的飯店吃西餐了。
　　……
羅絲
3月1日

3. "物美价廉 (物美價廉)" in this letter means _____ .

    (A) Chinese food in China looks good and is very cheap

    (B) Chinese food in the United States looks good but is very expensive

    (C) Chinese food in China is delicious and very cheap

    (D) Chinese food in the United States is delicious and very cheap

4. Why doesn't Rose eat Western food in China very often?

    (A) Because she prefers Chinese food to Western food.

    (B) Because she thinks that Western food in China is too expensive.

    (C) Because the variety of Western food in China is too limited.

    (D) Because she thinks that Western food in China is quite different from that in the United States.

5. How does Rose feel about her stay in China so far?

    (A) She misses Western food.

    (B) She needs more time to adjust.

    (C) She enjoys life in China.

    (D) She misses her parents a lot.

Read this advertisement.

[Simplified-character version]	[Traditional-character version]
店庆优惠　万勿错过	店慶優惠　萬勿錯過
为庆祝本店成立三周年，本月5日~15日所有消费享有8.8折的优惠（酒水、主食除外），每次消费达100元送30元午餐券或20元晚餐券。 　　欢迎您的光临!	爲慶祝本店成立三周年，本月5日~15日所有消費享有8.8折的優惠（酒水、主食除外），每次消費達100元送30元午餐券或20元晚餐券。 　　歡迎您的光臨!

6. This advertisement is for _____ .

    (A) a teahouse

    (B) a bar

    (C) a restaurant

    (D) a snack bar

7. For which of the following would you receive a 12% discount?

   (A) A glass of orange juice

   (B) A bowl of rice

   (C) A glass of wine

   (D) A steamed fish

8. If a person eats here twice and spends 100 *yuan* in total, _____ .

   (A) they can get a 30 *yuan* lunch ticket

   (B) they can get a 20 *yuan* supper ticket

   (C) they can get a 30 *yuan* lunch ticket or a 20 *yuan* supper ticket

   (D) they don't get any lunch or supper ticket

Read this story.

[Simplified-character version]	[Traditional-character version]
苏东坡（1037年–1101年），中国古代著名的诗人。他不仅诗写得好，而且也做得一手好菜。他创造出来的一道菜味道极美，人们为了纪念他，就把这道菜称作"东坡肉"。说起东坡肉，据说还有一个特殊的来历。 　　苏东坡那时是杭州的官员，为当地老百姓做了很多好事。老百姓听说苏东坡喜欢吃肉，到了快过年的时候，送了很多猪肉给他。苏东坡收到这么多猪肉，觉得应该和老百姓一起吃，于是他让家人把肉切成方块形，烧熟以后把这些肉和酒一起送到每家每户。他的家人在烧煮这道菜的时候，把"和酒一起送"听成了"和酒一起烧"，结果烧制出来的肉味美可口，非常好吃。从此，这种把肉和酒一起烧的方法就成了"东坡肉"的独特做法了。	蘇東坡（1037年–1101年），中國古代著名的詩人。他不僅詩寫得好，而且也做得一手好菜。他創造出來的一道菜味道極美，人們爲了紀念他，就把這道菜稱作"東坡肉"。説起東坡肉，據説還有一個特殊的來歷。 　　蘇東坡那時是杭州的官員，爲當地老百姓做了很多好事。老百姓聽説蘇東坡喜歡吃肉，到了快過年的時候，送了很多豬肉給他。蘇東坡收到這麼多豬肉，覺得應該和老百姓一起吃，於是他讓家人把肉切成方塊形，燒熟以後把這些肉和酒一起送到每家每户。他的家人在燒煮這道菜的時候，把"和酒一起送"聽成了"和酒一起燒"，結果燒製出來的肉味美可口，非常好吃。從此，這種把肉和酒一起燒的方法就成了"東坡肉"的獨特做法了。

9. Why did the local people send pork to Su Dongpo?

   (A) Because Su Dongpo was a famous chef.

   (B) Because they had a lot of pork.

   (C) Because Su Dongpo would pay them a good price.

   (D) Because they wanted to thank him.

10. Which of the following statements is TRUE?

    (A) "东坡肉 (東坡肉)" was created in honor of Su Dongpo's family.

    (B) "东坡肉 (東坡肉)" is round in shape.

    (C) "东坡肉 (東坡肉)" was created by Su Dongpo on purpose.

    (D) The main ingredients of "东坡肉 (東坡肉)" are pork and wine.

Read this passage.

[Simplified-character version]	[Traditional-character version]
中国人请客、吃饭的时候很讲究座位的安排。一般来说，正对着门的座位是上座；如果两人并排坐着的时候，通常以右为上座，以左为下座，这是因为中餐上菜时多以顺时针为上菜的方向，坐在右边的人比坐在左边的人能先夹到菜。中国人有推让座位的习惯，大家会请年纪大或地位高的人坐上座。上菜的时候一般先上肉菜，再上素菜，最后上汤，有时快吃完的时候也习惯上一些小点心。付费时，中国人没有各付各的习惯，一般由请客的人付钱。	中國人請客、吃飯的時候很講究座位的安排。一般來說，正對著門的座位是上座；如果兩人並排坐著的時候，通常以右爲上座，以左爲下座，這是因爲中餐上菜時多以順時針爲上菜的方向，坐在右邊的人比坐在左邊的人能先夾到菜。中國人有推讓座位的習慣，大家會請年紀大或地位高的人坐上座。上菜的時候一般先上肉菜，再上素菜，最後上湯，有時快吃完的時候也習慣上一些小點心。付費時，中國人沒有各付各的習慣，一般由請客的人付錢。

11. According to the passage, which of the following is the seat of honor?

    (A) The seat of the person paying the bill.

    (B) The seat on the left of the person paying the bill.

    (C) The seat closest to the door.

    (D) The seat directly facing the door.

12. According to the passage, which of these statements is TRUE?

    (A) In Chinese meals, soup is served before the vegetable dishes.

    (B) In Chinese meals, vegetable dishes are served last.

    (C) In Chinese meals, soup is served first.

    (D) In Chinese meals, meat dishes are followed by vegetable dishes.

Read this e-mail.

```
[_][□][X]

File   Edit   View   Insert   Format   Tools   Message   Help
New  |  Send  |  Foward  |  🖨  🖻  🖹  |  ▼  |  🖻  🖹  X  |  ✦ ▾ ✦ ▾ A⁺  |  🌐
```

[Simplified-character version]	[Traditional-character version]
发信人: 小高 收信人: 小明 主　题: 北京烤鸭真好吃!	發信人: 小高 收信人: 小明 主　題: 北京烤鴨真好吃!
小明: 　　你好! 好久没和你联系了, 最近过得怎么样? 　　我来北京三天了, 参观了不少名胜古迹, 也吃到了不少好吃的东西, 其中给我印象最深的是北京烤鸭, 可真好吃! 前天我去了北京最有名的全聚德烤鸭店吃烤鸭。点完菜没多久, 烤鸭就送过来了。厨师当场把鸭肉片成一片一片的, 速度非常快, 真令我们惊讶。烤鸭片完后, 我们就开始吃了: 先用筷子夹两三片烤鸭, 蘸一点酱, 放在一张很薄的饼上, 然后夹一点黄瓜和葱丝放在烤鸭上, 再把饼卷起来一起吃。北京烤鸭温热香脆, 肥而不腻, 确实可口。我下次还要去全聚德吃北京烤鸭。差点忘了告诉你, 我们吃完后, 服务员给了我一张明信片, 上面记录了我吃的烤鸭号: 全聚德第15405876只烤鸭! 　　你来北京的时候, 可别忘了吃北京烤鸭! 　　　　　　　　　　小高 　　　　　　　　　　1月4日	小明: 　　你好! 好久没和你聯繫了, 最近過得怎麼樣? 　　我来北京三天了, 參觀了不少名勝古蹟, 也吃到了不少好吃的東西, 其中给我印象最深的是北京烤鴨, 可真好吃! 前天我去了北京最有名的全聚德烤鴨店吃烤鴨。點完菜没多久, 烤鴨就送過來了。厨師當場把鴨肉片成一片一片的, 速度非常快, 真令我們驚訝。烤鴨片完後, 我們就開始吃了: 先用筷子夾兩三片烤鴨, 蘸一點醬, 放在一張很薄的餅上, 然後夾一點黃瓜和葱絲放在烤鴨上, 再把餅卷起來一起吃。北京烤鴨溫熱香脆, 肥而不膩, 確實可口。我下次還要去全聚德吃北京烤鴨。差點忘了告訴你, 我們吃完後, 服務員給了我一張明信片, 上面記錄了我吃的烤鴨號: 全聚德第15405876隻烤鴨! 　　你來北京的時候, 可別忘了吃北京烤鴨! 　　　　　　　　　　小高 　　　　　　　　　　1月4日

13. Which of the following statements is TRUE?

(A) Xiao Gao often contacts Xiao Ming.

(B) Xiao Gao came to Beijing in order to eat roast duck.

(C) Xiao Gao saw how a roast duck was cut into pieces.

(D) Xiao Gao went to the most famous restaurant in Beijing to eat roast duck yesterday.

14. Why did the waiter give Xiao Gao a postcard?

(A) So that Xiao Gao would remember the "number" of the roast duck he ate.

(B) So that Xiao Gao could send it to his friend in the United States.

(C) So that Xiao Gao would remember the sequence for eating roast duck.

(D) So that Xiao Gao would have something to remind him of the restaurant.

15. From the e-mail, we can infer that Xiao Gao _____ .

(A) is having a holiday in Beijing

(B) is on a business trip in Beijing

(C) is studying in Beijing

(D) is working in Beijing

Read this passage.

[Simplified-character version]	[Traditional-character version]
要想在北京吃到地道的小吃，最好去天安门附近的王府井小吃街。那儿不仅有北京的，还有中国其他地方的小吃，比方说新疆的羊肉串、陕西的羊肉泡馍、四川的麻辣粉、上海的小笼包等等。街上除了风味小吃以外，还有专门制作、销售民间工艺品的摊位，有的东西很便宜，但有的工艺品却非常贵。工艺品的好坏我分不出来，所以我尽量不买贵的，上次我买了一块玉，只花了三十元。在小吃街，如果逛累了，还可以停下来欣赏表演呢! 真是个有趣的好去处! 所以，你下次去天安门玩别忘了去王府井小吃街。	要想在北京吃到地道的小吃，最好去天安門附近的王府井小吃街。那兒不僅有北京的，還有中國其他地方的小吃，比方說新疆的羊肉串、陝西的羊肉泡饃、四川的麻辣粉、上海的小籠包等等。街上除了風味小吃以外，還有專門製作、銷售民間工藝品的攤位，有的東西很便宜，但有的工藝品卻非常貴。工藝品的好壞我分不出來，所以我儘量不買貴的，上次我買了一塊玉，只花了三十元。在小吃街，如果逛累了，還可以停下來欣賞表演呢! 真是個有趣的好去處! 所以，你下次去天安門玩別忘了去王府井小吃街。

16. According to the passage, what kind of snacks you can get in Wangfujing Snack Street?

(A) Beijing steamed pork dumpling

(B) Sichuan mutton cubes

(C) Xingjiang spicy bean noodles

(D) Snacks from Shanxi Province

17. Why does the author suggest "去天安门玩别忘了去王府井小吃街 (去天安門玩別忘了去王府井小吃街)"?

(A) Because Wangfujing Snack Street is conveniently located.

(B) Because Wangfujing Snack Street is an interesting place.

(C) Because the souvenirs sold at Wangfujing Snack Street are very cheap.

(D) Because there are free street performances at Wangfujing Snack Street.

Read this e-mail.

[Simplified-character version]	[Traditional-character version]
发信人: 儿子	發信人: 兒子
收信人: 爸爸	收信人: 爸爸
主　题: 听听您的意见	主　題: 聽聽您的意見

亲爱的爸爸:	親愛的爸爸:
您好!	您好!
本来想打电话给您, 但我怕电话里说不清楚, 所以就给您写信了。我们班下星期五要组织一场辩论赛, 辩论的题目是"故宫里可不可以开咖啡厅"。我们小组的观点是: 故宫里可以开咖啡厅。经过我们的讨论, 最后我们确定了以下几个理由:	本來想打電話給您, 但我怕電話裏説不清楚, 所以就給您寫信了。我們班下星期五要組織一場辯論賽, 辯論的題目是"故宫裏可不可以開咖啡廳"。我們小組的觀點是: 故宫裏可以開咖啡廳。經過我們的討論, 最後我們確定了以下幾個理由:
1. 故宫很大, 开咖啡厅可以给游客提供休息的地方;	1. 故宫很大, 開咖啡廳可以給遊客提供休息的地方;
2. 开咖啡厅赚来的钱可以用来维修故宫;	2. 開咖啡廳賺來的錢可以用來維修故宫;
3. 故宫很古老, 开咖啡厅也可以体现故宫现代化的一面。	3. 故宫很古老, 開咖啡廳也可以體現故宫現代化的一面。
我们想了很久, 只想到这三点, 总觉得不够, 所以写信给您, 想听听您的意见。明天是星期天, 我没有课, 如果您要打电话给我, 我晚上都会在家。期待您的回音。	我們想了很久, 只想到這三點, 總覺得不夠, 所以寫信給您, 想聽聽您的意見。明天是星期天, 我沒有課, 如果您要打電話給我, 我晚上都會在家。期待您的回音。
儿子陈杰	兒子陳傑
5月3日	5月3日

18. Why did Chen Jie write to his father instead of calling him?

(A) Because he had too much to say and did not want to spend a lot of money.

(B) Because it was not urgent; there was no need to make a phone call.

(C) Because the telephone line was not clear and he was afraid that his father wouldn't be able to hear him clearly.

(D) Because he had a lot to say and he was afraid that he couldn't explain himself properly on the telephone.

19. What is Chen Jie's attitude towards the debate next week?

(A) He is confident about winning the debate.

(B) He isn't very interested in it.

(C) He doesn't think he is fully prepared.

(D) He is very nervous about it.

20. The debate will be held on _____ .

(A) May 7

(B) May 8

(C) May 9

(D) May 10

Read this passage.

[Simplified-character version]	[Traditional-character version]
冬天是最适合吃火锅的季节，再加上好久没吃，嘴也馋了。正好今天周末，于是我打了几个电话邀朋友去一家老北京火锅店吃火锅。刚推开饭馆的门，就感觉到里面热气腾腾的，五六个人一桌一桌地围在一起吃，好不热闹。说起吃火锅，还确实是人越多越好，如果几个人在朋友家里吃，还能给主人省去很多麻烦：主人只要准备好材料，你想吃什么自己就涮什么，大家一块儿吃，不需要主人在厨房里一个人忙。真不知当初是谁发明了这么好的方法。	冬天是最適合吃火鍋的季節，再加上好久沒吃，嘴也饞了。正好今天週末，於是我打了幾個電話邀朋友去一家老北京火鍋店吃火鍋。剛推開飯館的門，就感覺到裏面熱氣騰騰的，五六個人一桌一桌地圍在一起吃，好不熱鬧。說起吃火鍋，還確實是人越多越好，如果幾個人在朋友家裏吃，還能給主人省去很多麻煩：主人只要準備好材料，你想吃什麼自己就涮什麼，大家一塊兒吃，不需要主人在厨房裏一個人忙。真不知當初是誰發明了這麼好的方法。

21. According to the passage, what is the MAIN reason the author asked his friends to eat hotpot?
    (A) His friends had invited him to have hotpot before.
    (B) He wanted to get together with his friends.
    (C) He hadn't eaten hotpot for a long time and felt like having it.
    (D) Because it was a weekend.

22. What does the author say about eating hotpot?
    (A) You should eat it at a restaurant together with friends or family.
    (B) It is very inexpensive to eat.
    (C) The best time to eat hotpot is during fall.
    (D) Eating hotpot is convenient and fun.

Read this public sign.

[Simplified-character version]

欢迎再次光临

[Traditional-character version]

歡迎再次光臨

23. Where would this sign most likely appear?
    (A) In a school
    (B) In a clinic
    (C) In a restaurant
    (D) In an office

24. What is the purpose of this sign?
    (A) To ask people to come again.
    (B) To thank people for coming.
    (C) To welcome people.
    (D) To ask people to wait patiently.

Read this public sign.

[Simplified-character version]

冷气开放

[Traditional-character version]

冷氣開放

25. Where would this sign most likely appear?
    (A) In a school
    (B) In a teahouse
    (C) In an office
    (D) In a hospital

Section Two

I.   Free Response (Writing)

Note: In this part, you may NOT move back and forth among questions.

Directions: You will be asked to write in Chinese in a variety of ways. In each case, you will be asked to write for a specific purpose and to a specific person. You should write in as complete and as culturally appropriate a manner as possible, taking into account the purpose and the person described.

1. Story Narration

The four pictures present a story. Imagine you are writing the story to a friend. Narrate a complete story as suggested by the pictures. Give your story a beginning, a middle, and an end.

2. Personal Letter

Imagine you received a letter from a Chinese pen pal. In the letter, he tells you that he likes eating Western fast food. However, his mother calls it junk food and prefers him to eat less of it. Sometimes, she doesn't even allow him to eat it at all. He is very upset and would like to discuss this topic with you. He wants to know whether fast food is popular in the United States, who eats it, and what your opinions are about it. Write a reply in letter format to discuss this topic.

3. E-Mail Response

Read this e-mail from a friend and then type a response.

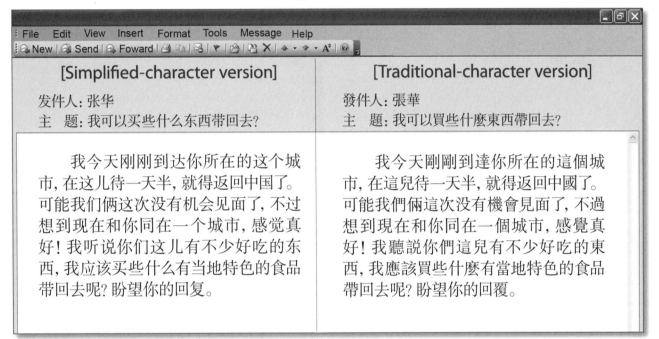

File   Edit   View   Insert   Format   Tools   Message   Help

New   Send   Foward

[Simplified-character version]	[Traditional-character version]
发件人: 张华	發件人: 張華
主　题: 我可以买些什么东西带回去?	主　题: 我可以買些什麼東西帶回去?
我今天刚刚到达你所在的这个城市, 在这儿待一天半, 就得返回中国了。可能我们俩这次没有机会见面了, 不过想到现在和你同在一个城市, 感觉真好! 我听说你们这儿有不少好吃的东西, 我应该买些什么有当地特色的食品带回去呢? 盼望你的回复。	我今天剛剛到達你所在的這個城市, 在這兒待一天半, 就得返回中國了。可能我們倆這次沒有機會見面了, 不過想到現在和你同在一個城市, 感覺真好! 我聽說你們這兒有不少好吃的東西, 我應該買些什麼有當地特色的食品帶回去呢? 盼望你的回覆。

4. Relay a Telephone Message

Imagine you are sharing an apartment with one of your classmates. One day you listen to a message for him on the answering machine. You will listen twice to the message. Then relay the message, including the important details, by typing a note to your classmate.

II. Free Response (Speaking)

Note: In this part, you may NOT move back and forth among questions.

Directions: You will participate in a simulated conversation. Each time it is your turn to speak, you will have 20 seconds to record. You should respond as fully and as appropriately as possible.

1. Conversation

Imagine you had dinner with your Chinese friend. Afterwards, you have a conversation with him about the meal you just ate together.

Directions: You will be asked to speak in Chinese on different topics in the following two questions. In each case, imagine you are making an oral presentation to your family in Chinese. First, you will read and hear the topic for your presentation. You will have 4 minutes to prepare your presentation. Then you will have 2 minutes to record your presentation. Your presentation should be as complete as possible.

2. Cultural Presentation

In your presentation, talk about your opinion of Chinese cuisine and the Chinese style of eating (chopsticks, etc.).

3. Event Plan

You have the opportunity to invite your classmates over for dinner. Discuss your plan with your family. Talk about what you need to buy and what you need to cook.

UNIT TWO
LESSON 4

Food and Fashion
What Should a Bridesmaid Wear?

Section One

I. Multiple Choice (Listen to the dialogs)

Note: In this part, you may NOT move back and forth among questions.

Directions: In this part, you will hear several short conversations or parts of conversations followed by four choices, designated (A), (B), (C), and (D). Choose the one that continues or completes the conversation in a logical and culturally appropriate manner. You will have 5 seconds to answer each question.

1.	(A)	(B)	(C)	(D)	5.	(A)	(B)	(C)	(D)
2.	(A)	(B)	(C)	(D)	6.	(A)	(B)	(C)	(D)
3.	(A)	(B)	(C)	(D)	7.	(A)	(B)	(C)	(D)
4.	(A)	(B)	(C)	(D)	8.	(A)	(B)	(C)	(D)

II. Multiple Choice (Listen to the selections)

Note: In this part, you may move back and forth only among the questions associated with the current listening selection.

Directions: In this part, you will listen to several selections in Chinese. For each selection, you will be told whether it will be played once or twice. You may take notes as you listen. After listening to each selection, you will see questions in English. For each question, choose the response that is best according to the selection. You will have 12 seconds to answer each question.

Selection 1

1. The group speaking has investigated _____ .
   (A) what kind of clothes students like to wear these days
   (B) opinions of parents and students on fashion
   (C) current fashion trends
   (D) what kind of clothes female students like to wear these days

2. The speaker is probably _____ .

   (A) a student

   (B) a teacher

   (C) a parent

   (D) a professional in the fashion industry

3. When was the survey conducted?

   (A) During the evenings of the previous week

   (B) On the weekend

   (C) During the summer vacation

   (D) During the previous semester

Selection 2

4. Which of the following does the saleswoman say about this brand of clothing?

   (A) It has a nice range of colors and styles.

   (B) It is very inexpensive.

   (C) The sizes are larger than those of other brands.

   (D) It is very popular with young people right now.

5. Which of the following statements is TRUE?

   (A) The man wasn't satisfied with the woman's service.

   (B) The man bought the "S" size item.

   (C) The man left the shop without buying anything.

   (D) The man tried on three different sizes of clothes.

Selection 3

6. Who asked Chen Yuan to call Li Yan?

   (A) Her parents

   (B) Her teacher

   (C) Her sister

   (D) Her classmate

7. Which of the following does Chen Yuan specifically ask Li Yan NOT to wear?

   (A) A white shirt

   (B) Jewelry

   (C) A dress

   (D) Jeans

8. What reason does Chen Yuan give for asking Li Yan to dress formally?
    (A) She says Li Yan looks better in formal clothes.
    (B) She encourages Li Yan to try something different.
    (C) She thinks the party tomorrow night will be very formal.
    (D) She doesn't want to be the only one who dresses formally at the party.

Selection 4

9. The two people are probably _____ .
    (A) a shop assistant and a customer
    (B) boyfriend and girlfriend
    (C) an employee and her manager
    (D) classmates

10. Did the woman buy anything in the end?
    (A) Yes, she bought 30 items of clothing.
    (B) Yes, she bought a sweater.
    (C) No, she didn't buy anything.
    (D) Yes, she bought some dresses.

11. We can infer from the text that the man's attitude is _____ .
    (A) polite
    (B) considerate
    (C) cautious
    (D) impatient

Selection 5

12. What do the girls in the show have in common?
    (A) They all have short hair.
    (B) They are all dressed like boys.
    (C) They are all wearing suits.
    (D) They are all wearing dresses.

13. What do the boys in the show have in common?
    (A) They all have colored hair.
    (B) They are all wearing jeans.
    (C) They are all wearing suits.
    (D) They are all very tall.

14. What is the event most likely to be?

    (A) A fashion show at a school   **(B)** A modeling competition

    (C) A fashion design competition   **(D)** A talent show

Selection 6

15. Which specific request does the girl make to the hairdresser?

    (A) To cut her hair short like a boy's.   **(B)** To perm her hair.

    (C) To dye her hair.   **(D)** To cut her hair just above her ears.

16. Why does the girl want to have a different hairstyle?

    (A) Her current hairstyle is not in fashion anymore.

    (B) She is bored of her current hairstyle.

    (C) She is having problems taking care of her current hairstyle.

    (D) Her current hairstyle is not allowed at her new school.

III. Multiple Choice (Reading)

Note: In this part, you may move back and forth among all the questions.

Directions: You will read several selections in Chinese. Each selection is accompanied by a number of questions in English. For each question, choose the response that is best according to the selection.

Read this notice.

[Simplified-character version]	[Traditional-character version]
欢迎您来到天美商场购物！为了庆祝元旦, 除一楼和六楼以外, 其他楼层所有商品8折出售, 活动时间从12月20号开始到1月20号。活动期间, 一次购物满500元将得到我们商场的一份精美的新年礼物。同时, 为了方便顾客购物, 我们商场从今天开始可以用信用卡消费。 　　下面介绍一下商场各层的情况: 一楼: 超市; 二楼: 童装; 三、四楼: 女装; 五楼: 男装; 六楼: 小吃城。祝大家购物愉快! 再次感谢您的光临! 　　　　　　　　　　　　天美商场 　　　　　　　　　　　　12月18日	歡迎您來到天美商場購物！爲了慶祝元旦, 除一樓和六樓以外, 其他樓層所有商品8折出售, 活動時間從12月20號開始到1月20號。活動期間, 一次購物滿500元將得到我們商場的一份精美的新年禮物。同時, 爲了方便顧客購物, 我們商場從今天開始可以用信用卡消費。 　　下面介紹一下商場各層的情況: 一樓: 超市; 二樓: 童裝; 三、四樓: 女裝; 五樓: 男裝; 六樓: 小吃城。祝大家購物愉快! 再次感謝您的光臨! 　　　　　　　　　　　　天美商場 　　　　　　　　　　　　12月18日

1. The special promotion is an activity to celebrate _____ .
   (A) Christmas
   (B) Thanksgiving
   (C) New Year
   (D) the opening of a shopping mall

2. Which of the following statements is TRUE?
   (A) Customers will receive a further discount if they spend over 500 *yuan*.
   (B) The restaurants are located on the 1st floor.
   (C) Customers will receive a 20% discount on any purchases made on the 3rd and 4th floors.
   (D) Credit card payments can be made only for purchases above 200 *yuan*.

3. How long will the promotion last?
   (A) Six weeks
   (B) One month
   (C) Two months
   (D) One week

Read this passage.

[Simplified-character version]

今天在上学的路上，我遇上了同学赵星，没想到我俩穿的衣服这么相似：都是一样的紫红色，款式也差不多。于是，我问赵星："你这件衣服在哪儿买的？"赵星告诉我："'秀水街'服装市场。买了好久了，一直都没穿，今天才第一次穿。"她看上去也特惊讶地问我："你的呢？"我摸了摸她的衣服，说："物美商场。昨天和我妈一块儿去买的，那儿不讲价，这件衣服350。""是吗？我这件衣服没你的贵。刚开始，老板也要350，后来我讲了价，200块钱。"不过赵星马上又说："商场的衣服一般来说比服装市场的质量好，尽管有时候衣服看起来差不多，但是多花点钱买质量好点的衣服还是很值得。"

[Traditional-character version]

今天在上學的路上，我遇上了同學趙星，沒想到我倆穿的衣服這麼相似：都是一樣的紫紅色，款式也差不多。於是，我問趙星："你這件衣服在哪兒買的？"趙星告訴我："'秀水街'服裝市場。買了好久了，一直都沒穿，今天才第一次穿。"她看上去也特驚訝地問我："你的呢？"我摸了摸她的衣服，說："物美商場。昨天和我媽一塊兒去買的，那兒不講價，這件衣服350。""是嗎？我這件衣服沒你的貴。剛開始，老板也要350，後來我講了價，200塊錢。"不過趙星馬上又說："商場的衣服一般來說比服裝市場的質量好，儘管有時候衣服看起來差不多，但是多花點錢買質量好點的衣服還是很值得。"

4. The clothes of the author and those of Zhao Xing are _____ .

   (A) almost the same in color, style, and price

   (B) almost the same in price, but the colors and the styles are different

   (C) almost the same in color and style, but the prices are different

   (D) completely different

5. What does Zhao Xing think is the difference between clothes bought at the market and clothes bought at the shopping mall?

   (A) Clothes from the shopping mall are cheaper and are of better quality.

   (B) Clothes from the shopping mall are cheaper but are of poorer quality.

   (C) Clothes from the shopping mall are more expensive but are of better quality.

   (D) Clothes from the shopping mall are more expensive and are of poorer quality.

Read this e-mail.

File   Edit   View   Insert   Format   Tools   Message   Help

New | Send | Foward |

[Simplified-character version]

发信人：李丽
收信人：张明
主　题：听听你们的意见

张明：

　　你好!

　　听说学校打算在中秋节那天举办一场晚会，要求每个班出一个节目。昨天你们讨论的时候我不在，后来听赵星说你们还没有商量好出什么节目。我这儿有个建议，你看行不行。我们班可以来个旗袍表演，一来我们班女生比男生多，她们几乎都有自己的旗袍，不需要再特意买；二来这个节目以前没有在学校的晚会上出现过，对大家来说一定很新鲜；再说，中秋节是一个传统的节日，我们在传统的节日上来个传统服装表演，这样更能增加节日的气氛。以上是我个人的想法，不知道你觉得怎么样？我还把信发给了班上其他的同学，明天我们上完第四节课后可以留下来再讨论讨论!

李丽
9月5日

[Traditional-character version]

發信人：李麗
收信人：張明
主　題：聽聽你們的意見

張明：

　　你好!

　　聽說學校打算在中秋節那天舉辦一場晚會，要求每個班出一個節目。昨天你們討論的時候我不在，後來聽趙星說你們還沒有商量好出什麼節目。我這兒有個建議，你看行不行。我們班可以來個旗袍表演，一來我們班女生比男生多，她們幾乎都有自己的旗袍，不需要再特意買；二來這個節目以前沒有在學校的晚會上出現過，對大家來說一定很新鮮；再說，中秋節是一個傳統的節日，我們在傳統的節日上來個傳統服裝表演，這樣更能增加節日的氣氛。以上是我個人的想法，不知道你覺得怎麼樣？我還把信發給了班上其他的同學，明天我們上完第四節課後可以留下來再討論討論!

李麗
9月5日

6. Why does Li Li write to Zhang Ming?
    (A) Because she wants to invite him to attend the class performance.
    (B) Because she wants to ask him to take part in the class performance.
    (C) Because she wants to tell him her idea for the class performance.
    (D) Because she wants to ask him about his ideas for the class performance.

7. What reason does Li Li give for suggesting a Cheongsam show?
    (A) The students do not have enough time to prepare for a grand class performance.
    (B) Most of the other girls in the class like the idea.
    (C) Li Li knows a sponsor who can lend them the Cheongsams.
    (D) There haven't been any Cheongsam shows in a school event before.

8. Which of the following statements is TRUE?
    (A) The e-mail was only sent to Zhang Ming.
    (B) Li Li is in charge of planning the performance.
    (C) The number of male and female students in the class is about the same.
    (D) Li Li suggests that they discuss the idea again during recess tomorrow.

Read this passage.

[Simplified-character version]	[Traditional-character version]
学校附近有一家做衣服的小店，小店里只有两个人，我们叫他们齐师傅和张阿姨。齐师傅今年快50了，在这个小店已经做了二十年，张阿姨还不到40岁，她嫁给齐师傅很久以后才开始学习做衣服。两口子过得虽不富裕，但他们每天看上去都特别开心。我们有时候衣服破了也去找他们帮助缝补，这时候张阿姨就会耐心地教我们，她也不担心我们学会了就不去她那儿了。不过，现在流行去商场买做好的成衣，我有时真担心哪天去那个小店就见不着他们了。不过，听张阿姨说，他们还会把店继续开下去，因为有很多老顾客很喜欢他们做的衣服。再说，他们走了，我们这些学生怎么办呢？	學校附近有一家做衣服的小店，小店裏只有兩個人，我們叫他們齊師傅和張阿姨。齊師傅今年快50了，在這個小店已經做了二十年，張阿姨還不到40歲，她嫁給齊師傅很久以後才開始學習做衣服。兩口子過得雖不富裕，但他們每天看上去都特別開心。我們有時候衣服破了也去找他們幫助縫補，這時候張阿姨就會耐心地教我們，她也不擔心我們學會了就不去她那兒了。不過，現在流行去商場買做好的成衣，我有時真擔心哪天去那個小店就見不著他們了。不過，聽張阿姨說，他們還會把店繼續開下去，因爲有很多老顧客很喜歡他們做的衣服。再說，他們走了，我們這些學生怎麼辦呢？

9. Which of the following statements concerning Aunt Zhang is TRUE?

   (A) She has worked in the same shop for 20 years.

   (B) She is the same age as her husband.

   (C) She is very kind to the students.

   (D) She is worried about the business because they are losing customers.

10. Why does the author sometimes worry about not seeing the couple any more?

    (A) Because Aunt Zhang has fallen ill.

    (B) Because Aunt Zhang is planning for her retirement.

    (C) Because Aunt Zhang might move overseas.

    (D) Because the couple may not be able to keep the business running.

11. According to the passage, why does Aunt Zhang decide to keep the business going?

    (A) Because there are still customers who like the clothes they make.

    (B) Because the students need help having their clothes mended.

    (C) Because she really enjoys making clothes.

    (D) Because they are reluctant to give up a business they have had for over 20 years.

Read this passage.

[Simplified-character version]	[Traditional-character version]
下周张杰要参加学校举办的题为"我长大了"的演讲比赛，张杰的爸妈这两天仍没决定让张杰穿什么衣服。张杰的妈妈认为，虽然是演讲，但孩子毕竟是孩子，跟大人不同，没有必要穿得太正式，只要穿一件平时的衣服，整齐干净、好看就行。可张杰的爸爸却不同意，他认为演讲是很正式的活动，在穿着上必须讲究，而且演讲比赛的题目正好是"我长大了"，穿一件小西装，和演讲的内容很符合。看着父母争来争去，没有结果，最后还是张杰自己说了话："你们也别争了，由我自己选择吧。但是现在还没法告诉你们，到时候再说吧。"	下週張傑要參加學校舉辦的題爲"我長大了"的演講比賽，張傑的爸媽這兩天仍没決定讓張傑穿什麼衣服。張傑的媽媽認爲，雖然是演講，但孩子畢竟是孩子，跟大人不同，没有必要穿得太正式，只要穿一件平時的衣服，整齊乾淨、好看就行。可張傑的爸爸卻不同意，他認爲演講是很正式的活動，在穿著上必須講究，而且演講比賽的題目正好是"我長大了"，穿一件小西裝，和演講的内容很符合。看著父母爭來爭去，没有結果，最後還是張傑自己説了話："你們也別爭了，由我自己選擇吧。但是現在還没法告訴你們，到時候再説吧。"

12. According to the passage, which of the following is TRUE?

    (A) The dress code for the speech contest has not yet been announced.

    (B) Zhang Jie thinks he should wear a suit to the speech contest.

    (C) Zhang Jie's mother wants to call his teacher to check on the dress code..

    (D) Zhang Jie's parents do not agree with each other about what he should wear.

13. Which of the following things does Zhang Jie's father say?

    (A) Casual clothes will not be appropriate for the contest.

    (B) What Zhang Jie usually wears doesn't look very good.

    (C) If wears a suit will make Zhang Jie stand out in the contest.

    (D) Zhang Jie should dress like an adult.

14. Which of the following can be inferred from the passage?

    (A) Zhang Jie has decided to wear a suit for the speech contest.

    (B) Zhang Jie is unhappy that his father is interfering with his decisions.

    (C) Zhang Jie will decide what to wear for the contest later.

    (D) Zhang Jie doesn't care about what he wears.

Read this information.

[Simplified-character version]

亲爱的同学们：
    你们好！
    我校服装设计兴趣小组已成立一年多了。在这段时间里，兴趣小组邀请了一些优秀的服装设计师为我们讲课，同学们也积极参加实践。现在我们的服装设计获得了很高的社会评价，比如，北京服装公司就准备与我校服装兴趣小组正式合作。另外，小组的部分同学在九月份参加了全国第一届学生服装设计大赛，获得了团体第二名的好成绩。这里展出的是参加这次比赛的作品，希望大家能喜欢。

                校服装设计小组
                10月8日

[Traditional-character version]

親愛的同學們：
    你們好！
    我校服裝設計興趣小組已成立一年多了。在這段時間裏，興趣小組邀請了一些優秀的服裝設計師為我們講課，同學們也積極參加實踐。現在我們的服裝設計獲得了很高的社會評價，比如，北京服裝公司就準備與我校服裝興趣小組正式合作。另外，小組的部分同學在九月份參加了全國第一届學生服裝設計大賽，獲得了團體第二名的好成績。這裏展出的是參加這次比賽的作品，希望大家能喜歡。

                校服裝設計小組
                10月8日

15. Which of the following statements is TRUE?

(A) A manager from the Beijing Fashion Company gave a lecture to the students.

(B) A member of the fashion design club won the first prize in a national contest.

(C) The Beijing Fashion Company helped the fashion design club to promote their designs.

(D) The designs of the fashion design club have been well received by the public.

16. The purpose of this message is to inform students about _____ .

(A) the first anniversary of the fashion design club

(B) an exhibition for the designs of the fashion design club

(C) a collaboration between the fashion design club and a group of professional fashion designers

(D) a recruitment drive the fashion design club is conducting now

17. The last sentence of the message "希望大家能喜欢（希望大家能喜歡）" is _____ .

(A) a suggestion   (B) a request

(C) a wish   (D) a warning

Read this passage.

[Simplified-character version]	[Traditional-character version]
中国北方的冬天比南方冷得多, 可赵芳却喜欢在中国的北方过冬。她认为北方虽然气温比较低, 可是冬天经常有阳光, 若是没风的天气, 阳光照在身上, 有一种暖洋洋的感觉。更重要的是, 北方室内有暖气, 一进屋就不用再穿棉衣, 只要穿着薄薄的、漂亮的毛衣就可以了。可是, 在南方就大不一样了。南方的大多数地方冬天经常下雨, 空气十分潮湿, 很多地方屋内也没有暖气, 必须经常穿着厚厚的衣服才行, 自然也就没有展示漂亮毛衣的机会了。	中國北方的冬天比南方冷得多, 可趙芳卻喜歡在中國的北方過冬。她認爲北方雖然氣溫比較低, 可是冬天經常有陽光, 若是没風的天氣, 陽光照在身上, 有一種暖洋洋的感覺。更重要的是, 北方室内有暖氣, 一進屋就不用再穿棉衣, 只要穿著薄薄的、漂亮的毛衣就可以了。可是, 在南方就大不一樣了。南方的大多數地方冬天經常下雨, 空氣十分潮濕, 很多地方屋内也没有暖氣, 必須經常穿著厚厚的衣服才行, 自然也就没有展示漂亮毛衣的機會了。

18. Zhao Fang thinks that the weather during winter in northern China _____ .

(A) is not as good as that of southern China but the temperature inside buildings is much higher

(B) is better than that of southern China and the temperature inside buildings is also much higher

(C) is not as good as that of southern China and the temperature inside buildings is also much lower

(D) is better than that of southern China but the temperature inside buildings is much lower

19. Why does Zhao Fang like winter in northern China?

    (A) Because she likes winter sports such as skiing.

    (B) Because she thinks winter in northern China is more comfortable than that in southern China.

    (C) Because she thinks winter in northern China is beautiful and not so windy.

    (D) Because she has lots of friends in northern China.

20. Which of the following statements can be inferred from the text?

    (A) It is common to have heating systems inside buildings in southern China.

    (B) People wear thin coats in winter in southern China.

    (C) Zhao Fang likes to wear light sweaters indoors during winter.

    (D) Zhao Fang does not like southern China at all.

Read this phrase.

[Simplified-character version]   [Traditional-character version]

请勿机洗   請勿機洗

21. Where would this phrase most likely appear?

    (A) a pair of shoes   **(B)** On bedsheets

    (C) On a silk dress   **(D)** On a cotton T-shirt

22. The purpose of this instruction is to remind people _____ .

    (A) you must not machine wash this item

    (B) you should soak this item before washing

    (C) you cannot use regular detergent to clean this item

    (D) you must use a brush to clean this item

Read this public sign.

[Simplified-character version]   [Traditional-character version]

一经售出，恕不退换   一經售出，恕不退換

23. Where would this sign most likely appear?

    (A) At a customer service counter   **(B)** In a car showroom

    (C) On a vending machine   **(D)** In a department store

24. The purpose of this sign is to inform people that _____ .

    (A) customers must pay for any product they break

    (B) store credit will be given for returned items

    (C) products that have been sold are not returnable

    (D) products labeled with this sign are already sold

Section Two

I. Free Response (Writing)

Note: In this part, you may NOT move back and forth among questions.

Directions: You will be asked to write in Chinese in a variety of ways. In each case, you will be asked to write for a specific purpose and to a specific person. You should write in as complete and as culturally appropriate a manner as possible, taking into account the purpose and the person described.

1. Story Narration

The four pictures present a story. Imagine you are writing the story to a friend. Narrate a complete story as suggested by the pictures. Give your story a beginning, a middle, and an end.

2. Personal Letter

Imagine you received a letter from a pen pal. The letter talks about your pen pal's favorite pop music and asks about pop singers you like and your taste in music. Write a reply in letter format. First, talk about the kinds of music that is generally popular in the United States these days. Then write about the kinds of music you like or dislike and why.

3. E-Mail Response

Read this e-mail from a friend and then type a response.

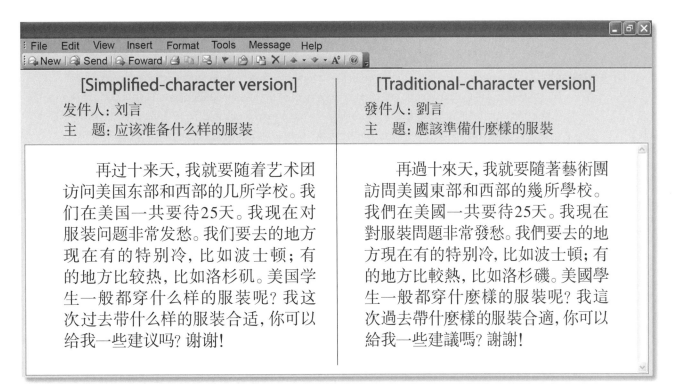

File   Edit   View   Insert   Format   Tools   Message   Help

New | Send | Foward |

[Simplified-character version]

发件人: 刘言
主　题: 应该准备什么样的服装

　　再过十来天, 我就要随着艺术团访问美国东部和西部的几所学校。我们在美国一共要待25天。我现在对服装问题非常发愁。我们要去的地方现在有的特别冷, 比如波士顿; 有的地方比较热, 比如洛杉矶。美国学生一般都穿什么样的服装呢? 我这次过去带什么样的服装合适, 你可以给我一些建议吗? 谢谢!

[Traditional-character version]

發件人: 劉言
主　題: 應該準備什麼樣的服裝

　　再過十來天, 我就要隨著藝術團訪問美國東部和西部的幾所學校。我們在美國一共要待25天。我現在對服裝問題非常發愁。我們要去的地方現在有的特別冷, 比如波士頓; 有的地方比較熱, 比如洛杉磯。美國學生一般都穿什麼樣的服裝呢? 我這次過去帶什麼樣的服裝合適, 你可以給我一些建議嗎? 謝謝!

4. Relay a Telephone Message

Imagine you arrive home one day and listen to a message from your sister to your mother. You will listen twice to the message. Then relay the message, including the important details, by typing a note to your mother.

II. Free Response (Speaking)

Note: In this part, you may NOT move back and forth among questions.

Directions: You will participate in a simulated conversation. Each time it is your turn to speak, you will have 20 seconds to record. You should respond as fully and as appropriately as possible.

1. Conversation

Imagine you have a guest visiting you today. You tell her about a party your class is planning to hold. You have a chat with her about the kind of clothes people should wear to this party.

Directions: You will be asked to speak in Chinese on different topics in the following two questions. In each case, imagine you are making an oral presentation to your class or your family in Chinese. First, you will read and hear the topic for your presentation. You will have 4 minutes to prepare your presentation. Then you will have 2 minutes to record your presentation. Your presentation should be as complete as possible.

2. Cultural Presentation

People of different cultures and nationalities have different understandings of the meaning of colors. In your presentation, describe the significance of the colors red, yellow, black, and white in Chinese culture.

3. Event Plan

You have the opportunity to attend a summer camp and need to pack your luggage. In your presentation, list the items you plan to pack and explain why you included them. This could include the purpose of the activity they will be used for, and the weather conditions at your destination.

UNIT THREE School and Family
LESSON 5 Chinese is Fun!

Section One

I. Multiple Choice (Listen to the dialogs)

Note: In this part, you may NOT move back and forth among questions.

Directions: In this part, you will hear several short conversations or parts of conversations followed by four choices, designated (A), (B), (C), and (D). Choose the one that continues or completes the conversation in a logical and culturally appropriate manner. You will have 5 seconds to answer each question.

1.	(A)	(B)	(C)	(D)	5.	(A)	(B)	(C)	(D)
2.	(A)	(B)	(C)	(D)	6.	(A)	(B)	(C)	(D)
3.	(A)	(B)	(C)	(D)	7.	(A)	(B)	(C)	(D)
4.	(A)	(B)	(C)	(D)	8.	(A)	(B)	(C)	(D)

II. Multiple Choice (Listen to the selections)

Note: In this part, you may move back and forth only among the questions associated with the current listening selection.

Directions: In this part, you will listen to several selections in Chinese. For each selection, you will be told whether it will be played once or twice. You may take notes as you listen. After listening to each selection, you will see questions in English. For each question, choose the response that is best according to the selection. You will have 12 seconds to answer each question.

Selection 1

1. Who is the speaker most likely to be?
   (A) The umpire
   (B) A member of the audience
   (C) A contestant
   (D) A cheerleader

2. In this game, what must you do to win?

(A) Win a set.

(B) Win two out of three sets.

(C) Win three out of five sets.

(D) Win five out of seven sets.

3. This game might be a _____ .

(A) volleyball game

(B) table tennis game

(C) badminton game

(D) tug-of-war game

Selection 2

4. What is the relationship between the two people?

(A) They are schoolmates in different classes.

(B) They are classmates.

(C) They are a teacher and a student.

(D) They are an aunt and a nephew.

5. Which of the following statements about the final score is TRUE?

(A) One team is one point ahead.

(B) One team is two points ahead.

(C) One team is three points ahead.

(D) The two teams are tied.

Selection 3

6. What does the man say about playing *Weiqi*?

(A) He knows nothing about it.

(B) He knows the rules but has never played it.

(C) He's already an expert at it.

(D) He has been playing it for a long time but isn't very good at it.

7. How did the man know that Wang Jing plays *Weiqi* very well?

(A) He learnt about Wang Jing's achievements on the Internet.

(B) He heard about Wang Jing's achievements from her friends.

(C) He attended the award ceremony of the *Weiqi* competition himself.

(D) He saw Wang Jing on TV.

Selection 4

8. According to the passage, which of the following statements about the 1-*yuan* coin is TRUE?
    (A) It is the thinnest of the Chinese coins.
    (B) It is the smallest of the Chinese coins.
    (C) It is the heaviest of the Chinese coins.
    (D) It is the lightest of the Chinese coins.

9. What is the main purpose of this speech?
    (A) To give a history of Chinese currency.
    (B) To give advice on how to save money.
    (C) To let people know how coins are made.
    (D) To let people know how to distinguish between different coins.

10. Which coins are mentioned in this speech?
    (A) The 1-*yuan* coin, 5-*jiao* coin, and 2-*jiao* coin.
    (B) The 2-*yuan* coin, 1-*yuan* coin, and 5-*jiao* coin.
    (C) The 5-*yuan* coin, 1-*yuan* coin, and 5-*jiao* coin.
    (D) The 1-*yuan* coin, 5-*jiao* coin, and 1-*jiao* coin.

Selection 5

11. How satisfied is the teacher with the students' performance in the first half of the semester?
    (A) Somewhat satisfied.
    (B) Very satisfied.
    (C) Not satisfied.
    (D) Very, very disappointed.

12. According to the teacher, what is most important in learning a foreign language?
    (A) The ability to speak confidently in front of others.
    (B) The discipline to study everyday.
    (C) The ability to remember vocabulary.
    (D) The habit of reading a lot.

13. What is the main difficulty faced by this group of students?
    (A) They don't know enough about the culture.
    (B) They are unable to understand the reading passages.
    (C) They find pronunciation rules too complex and difficult to master.
    (D) They feel awkward when they speak.

III. Multiple Choice (Reading)

Note: In this part, you may move back and forth among all the questions.

Directions: You will read several selections in Chinese. Each selection is accompanied by a number of questions in English. For each question, choose the response that is best according to the selection.

Read this e-mail.

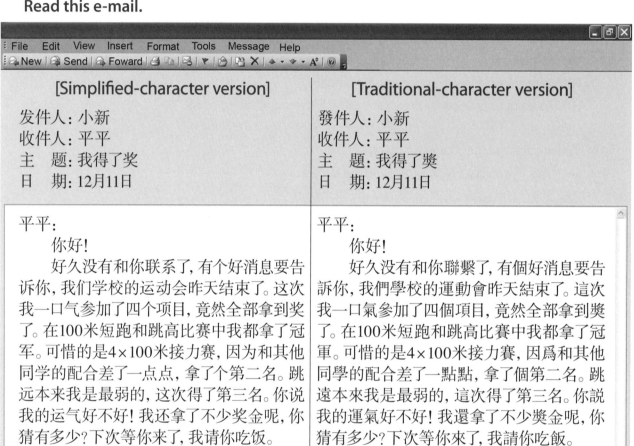

1. When did the sports meet end?

   (A) On December 8

   (B) On December 9

   (C) On December 10

   (D) On December 11

2. In how many events did Xiao Xin come second?

    (A) One

    (B) Two

    (C) Three

    (D) Four

Read this letter.

[Simplified-character version]

100810

小新:

    谢谢你给我订的蛋糕和寄来的礼物。我们班的同学都说你送给我的水果生日蛋糕好吃极了,你寄给我的那张CD我也很喜欢。前一阵子我花了很长时间,几乎跑遍了整个北京也没有找到这张CD。现在太好了。真的谢谢你!

    祝

学习进步!

寄: 北京大学汉语言文学系

陈新(收)

北京师范大学汉语文化学院 刘芳

小芳

2006−12−8   100875

[Traditional-character version]

100810

小新:

    謝謝你給我訂的蛋糕和寄來的禮物。我們班的同學都説你送給我的水果生日蛋糕好吃極了,你寄給我的那張CD我也很喜歡。前一陣子我花了很長時間,幾乎跑遍了整個北京也沒有找到這張CD。現在太好了。真的謝謝你!

    祝

學習進步!

寄: 北京大學漢語言文學系

陳新(收)

北京師範大學漢語文化學院 劉芳

小芳

2006−12−8   100875

3. Why did Chen Xin send Liu Fang a CD?

   (A) Because Chen Xin borrowed it from Liu Fang earlier.

   (B) Because it cannot be found in Beijing.

   (C) Because Liu Fang asked him to look for it.

   (D) Because it is Liu Fang's birthday.

4. Which of the following statements is TRUE?

   (A) It took Liu Fang a long time to find the CD.

   (B) Liu Fang hopes that Chen Xin will like the CD too.

   (C) Chen Xin is a student at Beijing Normal University.

   (D) Liu Fang studies Chinese at Beijing Normal University.

Read this poster.

[Simplified-character version]	[Traditional-character version]
主题: 神奇的基因工程 时间: 2007年3月17日晚7点 地点: 2号教学楼307教室 内容简介: 介绍基因工程的重大意义以及目前国内基因科学的发展状况 专家简介: 　　李力, 男, 汉族, 陕西人, 1947年10月出生。清华大学生命科学系教授。90年代以来, 一直从事基因工程研究, 参加并主持了多项国家级科研项目。同时也是人类基因计划项目的成员之一, 和国外科学家有着广泛的合作。在国内和国际多种重要刊物上发表了多篇文章, 影响很大。	主題: 神奇的基因工程 時間: 2007年3月17日晚7點 地點: 2號教學樓307教室 內容簡介: 介紹基因工程的重大意義以及目前國內基因科學的發展狀況 專家簡介: 　　李力, 男, 漢族, 陝西人, 1947年10月出生。清華大學生命科學系教授。90年代以來, 一直從事基因工程研究, 參加並主持了多項國家級科研項目。同時也是人類基因計劃項目的成員之一, 和國外科學家有著廣泛的合作。在國內和國際多種重要刊物上發表了多篇文章, 影響很大。

5. This is a poster about _____ .

   (A) a job vacancy

   (B) a movie

   (C) an interview

   (D) a lecture

6. What does "基因工程 (基因工程)" refer to?

   (A) It is a research method.

   (B) It is a research achievement.

   (C) It is an area of research.

   (D) It is an invention.

Read this message.

[Simplified-character version]

因明天（星期三）下午校学生会开会，网球协会的活动改为本周日下午三点进行。地点不变，还是在学校东边的网球场。如果你不能参加活动，一定要请假。可以打电话或者发电子邮件给我。请各位互相转告，谢谢！
田新

[Traditional-character version]

因明天（星期三）下午校學生會開會，網球協會的活動改爲本週日下午三點進行。地點不變，還是在學校東邊的網球場。如果你不能參加活動，一定要請假。可以直接發短信，也可以打電話或者發電子郵件給我。請各位互相轉告，謝謝！
田新

7. What is the objective of this text message?

   (A) To announce that the tennis club meeting will be at 2:00 pm.

   (B) To announce that the tennis club meeting has been postponed.

   (C) To announce that the venue for the tennis club meeting has been changed.

   (D) To announce that the tennis club meeting is going to start in 10 minutes.

8. Where will the tennis club meeting be held?

   (A) At the tennis court on the eastern side of the school.

   (B) At the eastern side of the tennis court.

   (C) At the school sports field.

   (D) At the school gym.

9. How many ways are there to ask for leave?

   (A) One

   (B) Two

   (C) Three

   (D) Four

Read this notice.

[Simplified-character version]	[Traditional-character version]
寻找学习伙伴	尋找學習伙伴
我是一名美国高中生，对汉语和中国文化很感兴趣。想找一个中国高中生（男女都可以）做我的学习伙伴，一起学习汉语和英语，交流彼此的想法。双方都不收任何的学习费用。除了周五下午以外，我每天下午两点以后都有时间。有意者请与我联系。 　　联系方式: 13366923317 杰森 2007年2月11日	我是一名美國高中生，對漢語和中國文化很感興趣。想找一個中國高中生（男女都可以）做我的學習伙伴，一起學習漢語和英語，交流彼此的想法。雙方都不收任何的學習費用。除了週五下午以外，我每天下午兩點以後都有時間。有意者請與我聯繫。 　　聯繫方式: 13366923317 傑森 2007年2月11日

10. What is the purpose of this notice?

    (A) To find a roommate.

    (B) To find a Chinese teacher.

    (C) To find a study partner.

    (D) To find a pen pal.

11. Jason will be available at _____ .

    (A) 3:00 pm, Friday

    (B) 1:00 pm, Friday

    (C) 1:00 pm, Monday

    (D) 3:00 pm, Tuesday

12. Which of the following statements is TRUE?

    (A) Jason prefers the person to be a Chinese male.

    (B) Jason expects the person to share the costs.

    (C) Jason is only available to take calls after 2:00 pm.

    (D) Jason is a senior high school student in the United States.

Read this passage.

[Simplified-character version]	[Traditional-character version]
来吧，发挥你的想像力与创造力 ——高中生绘画创作大赛火热报名中 参赛条件: 作者必须是在校高中生，至 　　　　　少提交一件亲手创作的作 　　　　　品，至多不超过三件 报名时间: 1月11日至1月12日 奖项设置: 一等奖　1 名　奖金1000元 　　　　　二等奖　2 名　奖金500元 　　　　　三等奖　3 名　奖金200元 　　　　　优秀奖　100名　奖金50元 　　所有参赛者都会获得一份精美 的礼品。期待你的参加! 　　　　　高中生绘画创作大赛组委会 　　　　　　　　　　　　　　1月5日	來吧，發揮你的想像力與創造力 ——高中生繪畫創作大賽火熱報名中 參賽條件: 作者必須是在校高中生，至 　　　　　少提交一件親手創作的作 　　　　　品，至多不超過三件 報名時間: 1月11日至1月12日 獎項設置: 一等獎　1 名　獎金1000元 　　　　　二等獎　2 名　獎金500元 　　　　　三等獎　3 名　獎金200元 　　　　　優秀獎　100名　獎金50元 　　所有參賽者都會獲得一份精美的 禮品。期待你的參加! 　　　　　高中生繪畫創作大賽組委會 　　　　　　　　　　　　　　1月5日

13. What is this poster about?

    (A) A painting contest

    (B) An essay writing contest

    (C) A poetry contest

    (D) A song writing contest

14. Who will take part in this activity?

    (A) Senior high school students

    (B) Primary school students

    (C) Undergraduates

    (D) Working adults

15. How many pieces of work can a person submit?

    (A) Up to three

    (B) Up to four

    (C) Up to five

    (D) As many as they like

16. If two pieces of your work win the second and fourth prize, you will get _____ .

    (A) 1200 *yuan* and a gift

    (B) 550 *yuan* and a gift

    (C) 700 *yuan* and a gift

    (D) 500 *yuan* and a gift

Read this passage.

[Simplified-character version]	[Traditional-character version]
我是一个高二的学生。我喜欢交朋友，特别喜欢和爱好相同的人交朋友。周末我多半会和朋友一起去看电影或者是去一些地方游览，偶尔也会去郊外玩。我一个人的时候，喜欢听音乐，但不是所有的音乐都听。拿流行音乐和古典音乐来比，我更愿意听古典音乐。我还喜欢画画，但它们都不是我最喜欢的，我最喜欢的是读书。	我是一個高二的學生。我喜歡交朋友，特別喜歡和愛好相同的人交朋友。週末我多半會和朋友一起去看電影或者是去一些地方遊覽，偶爾也會去郊外玩。我一個人的時候，喜歡聽音樂，但不是所有的音樂都聽。拿流行音樂和古典音樂來比，我更願意聽古典音樂。我還喜歡畫畫，但它們都不是我最喜歡的，我最喜歡的是讀書。

17. What does the author like to do when he is alone?

    (A) Watch movies

    (B) Listen to music

    (C) Paint

    (D) Read books

18. Which of the following statements about the author is TRUE?

    (A) He usually goes to the suburbs by himself on weekends.

    (B) His favorite hobby is painting.

    (C) He prefers pop music to classical music.

    (D) He likes making new friends.

Read this notice.

[Simplified-character version]

走进山区——伸出爱心之手

为了支持偏远地区的教育事业,帮助那些贫困山区不能上学的孩子,经学校研究,决定在全校学生中开展"我为山区献爱心"的捐助活动。

活动主题: 帮助别人,让自己快乐

捐助对象: 黄岗山区中学

活动参与人: 所有在校学生

活动形式: 学生以个人名义捐赠课本或课外读物。捐赠的书籍必须外观完好无损,书页整洁干净,最好是比较新的图书。

活动时间: 9月11日到12月20日

北京101中学
9月11日

[Traditional-character version]

走進山區——伸出愛心之手

爲了支持偏遠地區的教育事業,幫助那些貧困山區不能上學的孩子,經學校研究,決定在全校學生中開展"我爲山區獻愛心"的捐助活動。

活動主題: 幫助別人,讓自己快樂

捐助對象: 黃崗山區中學

活動參與人: 所有在校學生

活動形式: 學生以個人名義捐贈課本或課外讀物。捐贈的書籍必須外觀完好無損,書頁整潔乾淨,最好是比較新的圖書。

活動時間: 9月11日到12月20日

北京101中學
9月11日

19. What is the purpose of this activity?

(A) To give away unwanted books.

(B) To give students a chance to experience life in the mountains.

(C) To help poor children in mountain areas.

(D) To launch a program called "伸出爱心之手(伸出爱心之手)."

20. Who are the books donated to?

(A) Children in a mountain hospital

(B) The students of 101 High School

(C) Children in an orphanage

(D) High school students in the Huanggang mountain area

Read this public sign.

[Simplified-character version]

爱护花草，人人有责

[Traditional-character version]

愛護花草，人人有責

21. Where would this sign most likely appear?

   (A) On a lawn

   (B) At th beach

   (C) At a running track

   (D) In a forest

22. This sign is _____ .

   (A) a notice for a sports activity

   (B) an advertising slogan

   (C) a warning not to touch anything

   (D) a reminder for people to act responsibly

Section Two

I. Free Response (Writing)

Note: In this part, you may NOT move back and forth among questions.

Directions: You will be asked to write in Chinese in a variety of ways. In each case, you will be asked to write for a specific purpose and to a specific person. You should write in as complete and as culturally appropriate a manner as possible, taking into account the purpose and the person described.

1. Story Narration

The four pictures present a story. Imagine you are writing the story to a friend. Narrate a complete story as suggested by the pictures. Give your story a beginning, a middle, and an end.

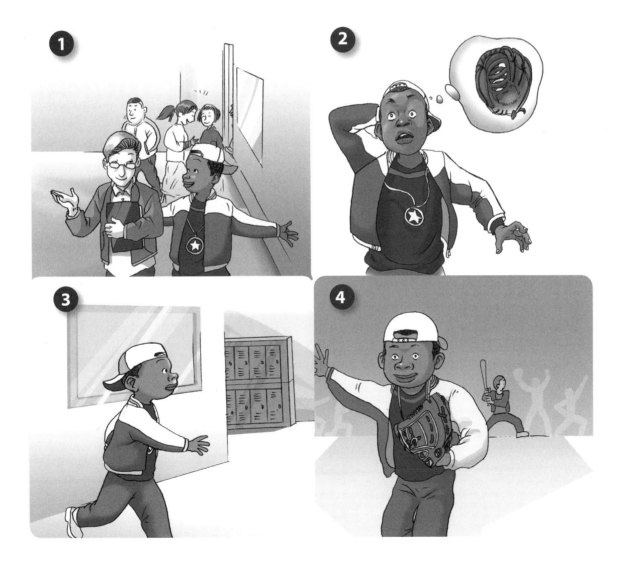

2. Personal Letter

Imagine you received a letter from a pen pal. He mentions that he spends most of his spare time playing video games. Write a reply in letter format. Write about the video games you have played or you know of, and your opinions of video games. Justify your opinion with specific reasons and examples.

3. E-Mail Response

Read this e-mail from a friend and then type a response.

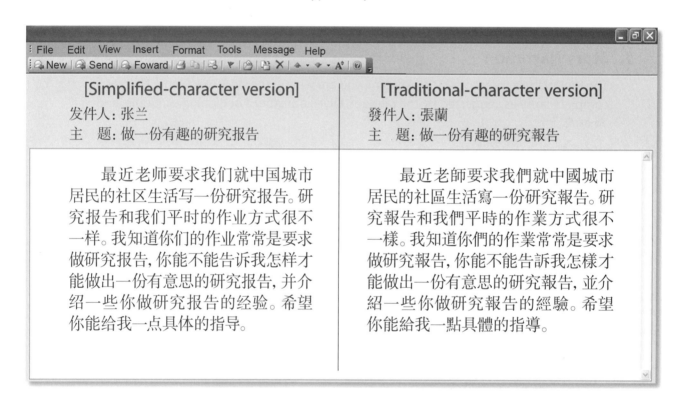

File   Edit   View   Insert   Format   Tools   Message   Help

New | Send | Foward | | | | | | | X | | | | | |

[Simplified-character version]

发件人: 张兰
主　题: 做一份有趣的研究报告

　　最近老师要求我们就中国城市居民的社区生活写一份研究报告。研究报告和我们平时的作业方式很不一样。我知道你们的作业常常是要求做研究报告，你能不能告诉我怎样才能做出一份有意思的研究报告，并介绍一些你做研究报告的经验。希望你能给我一点具体的指导。

[Traditional-character version]

發件人: 張蘭
主　題: 做一份有趣的研究報告

　　最近老師要求我們就中國城市居民的社區生活寫一份研究報告。研究報告和我們平時的作業方式很不一樣。我知道你們的作業常常是要求做研究報告，你能不能告訴我怎樣才能做出一份有意思的研究報告，並介紹一些你做研究報告的經驗。希望你能給我一點具體的指導。

4. Relay a Telephone Message

Imagine you are sharing an apartment with some Chinese friends. You arrive home one day and listen to a message on the answering machine. The message is for one of your Chinese friends. You will listen to the message twice.

Then relay the message, including the important details, by typing a rute to your friend.

II. Free Response (Speaking)

Note: In this part, you may NOT move back and forth among questions.

Directions: You will participate in a simulated conversation. Each time it is your turn to speak, you will have 20 seconds to record. You should respond as fully and as appropriately as possible.

1. Conversation

Recently, there have been some exchange students in your school. After class, you have a conversation with one of them about your opinions on your school and on education in general.

Directions: You will be asked to speak in Chinese on different topics in the following two questions. In each case, imagine you are making an oral presentation to your class in Chinese. First, you will read and hear the topic for your presentation. You will have 4 minutes to prepare your presentation. Then you will have 2 minutes to record your presentation. Your presentation should be as complete as possible.

2. Cultural Presentation

Find a school calendar from a senior high school in China on the Internet. In your presentation, describe the school's curriculum and other activities, including mid-term and end-of-term exams. Describe how many terms the school has, when these begin and end, and when the school vacations are. Also, compare this school calendar with yours.

3. Event Plan

Your class plans to buy some books. You have the opportunity to plan a fair to raise money to buy these books. In your presentation, explain the purpose of the fair, what you will sell, and why.

UNIT THREE
LESSON 6
School and Family
My Father, Laoshe

Section One

I. Multiple Choice (Listen to the dialogs)

Note: In this part, you may NOT move back and forth among questions.

Directions: In this part, you will hear several short conversations or parts of conversations followed by four choices, designated (A), (B), (C), and (D). Choose the one that continues or completes the conversation in a logical and culturally appropriate manner. You will have 5 seconds to answer each question.

1.	(A)	(B)	(C)	(D)	5.	(A)	(B)	(C)	(D)
2.	(A)	(B)	(C)	(D)	6.	(A)	(B)	(C)	(D)
3.	(A)	(B)	(C)	(D)	7.	(A)	(B)	(C)	(D)
4.	(A)	(B)	(C)	(D)	8.	(A)	(B)	(C)	(D)

II. Multiple Choice (Listen to the selections)

Note: In this part, you may move back and forth only among the questions associated with the current listening selection.

Directions: In this part, you will listen to several selections in Chinese. For each selection, you will be told whether it will be played once or twice. You may take notes as you listen. After listening to each selection, you will see questions in English. For each question, choose the response that is best according to the selection. You will have 12 seconds to answer each question.

Selection 1

1. What does the man think of the weather in Beijing?
   (A) He finds it too cold and dry.
   (B) He prefers it to the weather in Shanghai.
   (C) He doesn't like the way it changes all the time.
   (D) He likes it very much.

2. From the conversation, which of the following statements is most likely to be TRUE?
   (A) The woman has already lived in Beijing for more than three years.
   (B) The woman just arrived in Beijing last month.
   (C) The woman has never lived in Beijing.
   (D) The woman has lived in Beijing for one year.

Selection 2

3. Who is the speaker likely to be?
   (A) The teacher of this class
   (B) A student in this class
   (C) The school receptionist
   (D) One of the students' parents

4. How many issues are mentioned in this meeting?
   (A) One
   (B) Two
   (C) Three
   (D) Four

5. The parents need to write a letter after the meeting. What is this about?
   (A) Their children's health.
   (B) Their children's hobbies.
   (C) Their children's behavior at home.
   (D) Their children's names.

Selection 3

6. Who gave the boy his Chinese name?
   (A) His father.
   (B) His mother.
   (C) His Chinese friend.
   (D) It's not mentioned.

7. According to the conversation, which of the following statements is TRUE?
   (A) The woman thinks that all Chinese names have meaning.
   (B) The woman doesn't know the meaning of the man's name.
   (C) The man knows that every Chinese name has meaning.
   (D) The man knows the meaning of his Chinese name.

Selection 4

8. Where is the boy going?

    (A) To his school

    (B) On holiday overseas

    (C) To a friend's place

    (D) To a sports meeting

9. How does the boy feel about the woman?

    (A) He is very interested in her.

    (B) He is very impatient with her.

    (C) He is very worried about her.

    (D) He is very angry with her.

Selection 5

10. What does the woman say about watching a movie tonight?

    (A) She has time but she doesn't want to go.

    (B) She would like to go but is too busy.

    (C) She doesn't like movies and is busy anyway.

    (D) She might go but it depends on the kind of movie.

11. What does the man say about Chinese movies?

    (A) He doesn't like Chinese movies, especially martial arts movies.

    (B) He likes Chinese movies very much.

    (C) He likes some Chinese martial arts movies.

    (D) He doesn't like Bruce Lee's martial arts movies.

12. What does the woman think of Bruce Lee's martial arts movies?

    (A) She thinks they are very good.

    (B) She thinks they are too old and doesn't like them.

    (C) She thinks they are better than martial arts movies made recently.

    (D) She thinks they are too violent.

Selection 6

13. Where did Xiao Wang buy the sports clothes?

    (A) Off the Internet

    (B) From a nearby shop

    (C) From his younger brother

    (D) From his classmate

14. Why does the woman want to know where Xiao Wang bought his sports clothes?

  (A) She wants to buy the same clothes for her cousin.

  (B) She wants to buy the same clothes for her younger brother.

  (C) She wants to buy the same clothes for her boyfriend.

  (D) She wants to buy similar clothes for herself.

15. Why does the man like the sports clothes so much?

  (A) Because they are very cheap.

  (B) Because they are very comfortable.

  (C) Because they are very fashionable.

  (D) Because they have a photo of his favorite athlete printed on them.

III. Multiple Choice (Reading)

Note: In this part, you may move back and forth among all the questions.

Directions: You will read several selections in Chinese. Each selection is accompanied by a number of questions in English. For each question, choose the response that is best according to the selection.

Read this note.

[Simplified-character version]

甜甜：

    妈妈要去出差，后天才能回来，妈妈不在家的这几天，你一定要记得吃早餐，不然又会胃疼了。今天的菜已经放在冰箱里了，你只要拿出来放到锅里热一下就可以了，吃完以后一定要洗碗。另外，齐阿姨明天晚上会来我们家，她从外地旅游回来，给我们带了一些东西，你把她的笔记本电脑还给她。有什么事儿就给妈妈打电话。

               妈妈
               5月4日

[Traditional-character version]

甜甜：

    媽媽要去出差，後天才能回來，媽媽不在家的這幾天，你一定要記得吃早餐，不然又會胃疼了。今天的菜已經放在冰箱裏了，你只要拿出來放到鍋裏熱一下就可以了，吃完以後一定要洗碗。另外，齊阿姨明天晚上會來我們家，她從外地旅遊回來，給我們帶了一些東西，你把她的筆記本電腦還給她。有什麼事兒就給媽媽打電話。

               媽媽
               5月4日

1. When would Tiantian's mother probably come back?

    (A) On May 5

    (B) On May 6

    (C) On May 7

    (D) On May 8

2. Which of the following can we infer from the passage?

    (A) Tiantian doesn't eat supper often.

    (B) Tiantian likes to eat a lot.

    (C) Tiantian always washes the dishes.

    (D) Tiantian doesn't eat breakfast often.

3. Which of the following statements about Aunt Qi is TRUE?

    (A) She works in a computer company.

    (B) Her daughter is Tiantian's classmate.

    (C) She bought Tiantian a computer.

    (D) She has just returned from her vacation.

Read this passage.

[Simplified-character version]	[Traditional-character version]
每个中国人都有自己的姓，这些姓有不同的来历，比如说，有的是从古代国家的名字发展来的，比如有陈国、吴国、赵国，后来有了陈姓、吴姓和赵姓；有的和从事的工作有关，如陶姓的祖先是做陶器的……过去人们常常说"张、王、李、赵，遍地刘"，意思是说在中国，姓这些姓的人特别多。根据最新的统计，全中国姓"李"的人最多。	每個中國人都有自己的姓，這些姓有不同的來歷，比如說，有的是從古代國家的名字發展來的，比如有陳國、吳國、趙國，後來有了陳姓、吳姓和趙姓；有的和從事的工作有關，如陶姓的祖先是做陶器的……過去人們常常說"張、王、李、趙，遍地劉"，意思是說在中國，姓這些姓的人特別多。根據最新的統計，全中國姓"李"的人最多。

4. If a person's family name is Tao, it is probably because _____ .

    (A) their ancestors made pottery

    (B) their ancestors were government officials

    (C) their ancestors came from a town called Tao

    (D) their ancestors might not be from China originally

5. According to the passage, people with the family name "Li" _____ .

   (A) are fewer in number than people with the family name "Liu"

   (B) have ancestors who came from a town called Li

   (C) are greater in number than people with the family name "Zhao"

   (D) have ancestors who specialized in planting fruit

Read this diary.

[Simplified-character version]	[Traditional-character version]
我会常常幻想自己的未来,十年后的我会在哪儿,在做什么工作,会和什么样的人结婚呢? 我想我会一直读书,要拿更高的学位,这也是爸爸妈妈对我的期望。将来上大学我想念计算机系或者是经济系,因为我对电脑和赚钱都有很大的兴趣。毕业以后我想开一家公司。我也希望到中国学习中文,看中国的电影,了解中国的文化。我想我可以一面学习中文,一面教中国人英文,因为中国有很多人都想学习英文,这样做不是一举两得吗? 我还想到世界各地去旅行,了解欧洲古老的文化,去看看可爱的亚洲风光和美丽的大沙漠。我觉得旅行不但能使身心愉快,也是增长知识的好方法。	我會常常幻想自己的未來,十年後的我會在哪兒,在做什麼工作,會和什麼樣的人結婚呢? 我想我會一直讀書,要拿更高的學位,這也是爸爸媽媽對我的期望。將來上大學我想念計算機系或者是經濟系,因爲我對電腦和賺錢都有很大的興趣。畢業以後我想開一家公司。我也希望到中國學習中文,看中國的電影,瞭解中國的文化。我想我可以一面學習中文,一面教中國人英文,因爲中國有很多人都想學習英文,這樣做不是一舉兩得嗎? 我還想到世界各地去旅行,瞭解歐洲古老的文化,去看看可愛的亞洲風光和美麗的大沙漠。我覺得旅行不但能使身心愉快,也是增長知識的好方法。

6. According to the diary, what does the author want to do in the future?

   (A) He wants to become a doctor.

   (B) He wants to become a reporter.

   (C) He wants to set up his own company.

   (D) He wants to become a university lecturer.

7. Why does the author want to travel all over the world when he grows up?

   (A) Because he wants to get away from his family.

   (B) Because he wants to make more friends.

   (C) Because he wants to learn different languages.

   (D) Because he wants to have the chance to broaden his horizons.

8. According to the diary, what do the author's parents hope that he will do?

   (A) They hope that he will attain high academic qualifications.

   (B) They hope that he will study computer science.

   (C) They hope that he will become a university lecturer.

   (D) They hope that he will become an economist.

Read this e-mail.

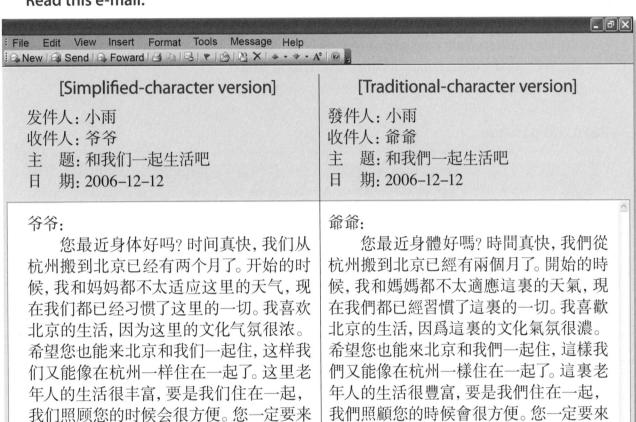

[Simplified-character version]

发件人: 小雨
收件人: 爷爷
主　题: 和我们一起生活吧
日　期: 2006–12–12

爷爷:

　　您最近身体好吗? 时间真快, 我们从杭州搬到北京已经有两个月了。开始的时候, 我和妈妈都不太适应这里的天气, 现在我们都已经习惯了这里的一切。我喜欢北京的生活, 因为这里的文化气氛很浓。希望您也能来北京和我们一起住, 这样我们又能像在杭州一样住在一起了。这里老年人的生活很丰富, 要是我们住在一起, 我们照顾您的时候会很方便。您一定要来呀。

　　　祝
身体健康!

　　　　　　　　　　　　小雨

[Traditional-character version]

發件人: 小雨
收件人: 爺爺
主　題: 和我們一起生活吧
日　期: 2006–12–12

爺爺:

　　您最近身體好嗎? 時間真快, 我們從杭州搬到北京已經有兩個月了。開始的時候, 我和媽媽都不太適應這裏的天氣, 現在我們都已經習慣了這裏的一切。我喜歡北京的生活, 因爲這裏的文化氣氛很濃。希望您也能來北京和我們一起住, 這樣我們又能像在杭州一樣住在一起了。這裏老年人的生活很豐富, 要是我們住在一起, 我們照顧您的時候會很方便。您一定要來呀。

　　　祝
身體健康!

　　　　　　　　　　　　小雨

9. According to the e-mail, which of the following statements is TRUE?

   (A) Xiao Yu's father hasn't adapted to life in Beijing.

   (B) Xiao Yu's mother doesn't like living in Beijing.

   (C) Xiao Yu and her mother couldn't get used to Beijing's weather at first.

   (D) Senior citizens in Beijing lead boring lives.

10. Why does Xiao Yu say she likes living in Beijing?

    (A) Because there are many historical places in Beijing.

    (B) Because she likes modern cities.

    (C) Because the nightlife in Beijing is good.

    (D) Because Beijing is a culturally rich city.

11. Why did Xiao Yu write this letter?

    (A) Because her grandfather asked her to write about her life in Beijing.

    (B) Because her grandfather is feeling lonely in Hangzhou.

    (C) Because she wants her grandfather to visit her in Beijing.

    (D) Because she wants her grandfather to move to Beijing.

Read this passage.

[Simplified-character version]	[Traditional-character version]
上午八点半，妈妈把苗苗叫醒了，"苗苗，快起床！""让我再睡一会儿啊。"苗苗半闭着眼睛说道。"再不起床就要迟到了。"妈妈接着说。"迟到也没关系嘛，今天是星期天。"苗苗还是不想马上起床。"赶快！你看隔壁小兰，昨天上计算机辅导班，今天上数学辅导班，晚上还有音乐课，你才上了几个班啊。"妈妈说着有些生气了。"可是，一个数学班就够多了。"苗苗答道。"孩子呀，要是现在不好好学习，将来别人都比你强，你怎么办呢？现在有机会，就要抓紧学习，不要浪费时间。"妈妈说完后，把苗苗从床上拉了起来。	上午八點半，媽媽把苗苗叫醒了，"苗苗，快起床！""讓我再睡一會兒啊。"苗苗半閉著眼睛說道。"再不起床就要遲到了。"媽媽接著說。"遲到也沒關係嘛，今天是星期天。"苗苗還是不想馬上起床。"趕快！你看隔壁小蘭，昨天上計算機輔導班，今天上數學輔導班，晚上還有音樂課，你才上了幾個班啊。"媽媽說著有些生氣了。"可是，一個數學班就夠多了。"苗苗答道。"孩子呀，要是現在不好好學習，將來別人都比你強，你怎麼辦呢？現在有機會，就要抓緊學習，不要浪費時間。"媽媽說完後，把苗苗從床上拉了起來。

12. Why did Miaomiao's mother wake her up?

    (A) She had to see a doctor.

    (B) She had to go to the library.

    (C) She had to go for computer class.

    (D) She had to go for math class.

13. Why didn't Miaomiao want to get up?
    (A) Because she wanted to sleep longer.
    (B) Because she was in a bad mood.
    (C) Because she did not sleep well the night before.
    (D) Because she was not feeling well.

14. Which of the following statements about Xiao Lan is TRUE?
    (A) She is Miaomiao's cousin.
    (B) She was top of the class last semester.
    (C) She has tennis lessons every weekend.
    (D) She goes for computer class on Saturdays.

15. From the passage, we can infer that Miaomiao's mother thinks that _____ .
    (A) Miaomiao is doing poorly in school.
    (B) Miaomiao is doing very well in school.
    (C) Miaomiao's grades will improve because of her weekend classes.
    (D) Miaomiao is lazier than she used to be.

Read this passage.

[Simplified-character version]	[Traditional-character version]
以前, 中国人祖孙三代十几口人生活在一起, 是很平常的事情。尤其是在农村, 人们靠种田养活自己, 家里人越多, 那么收入也会越多。但是现在的情况发生了很大的变化, 尤其是在城市里。家庭人数的多少和家庭收入关系不大。现在城市里的年轻人很难想像以前那种大家庭的生活, 一大家人吃住在一起, 怎么可能有个人的空间呢? 现在的城市住房越来越紧张, 看来, 中国人以前大家庭的居住方式在大城市里会渐渐成为历史。	以前, 中國人祖孫三代十幾口人生活在一起, 是很平常的事情。尤其是在農村, 人們靠種田養活自己, 家裏人越多, 那麼收入也會越多。但是現在的情況發生了很大的變化, 尤其是在城市裏。家庭人數的多少和家庭收入關係不大。現在城市裏的年輕人很難想像以前那種大家庭的生活, 一大家人吃住在一起, 怎麼可能有個人的空間呢? 現在的城市住房越來越緊張, 看來, 中國人以前大家庭的居住方式在大城市裏會漸漸成爲歷史。

16. According to the passage, many young people living in big cities these days _____ .

    (A) like staying in apartments

    (B) like to live with their parents

    (C) prefer not to live in a large family group

    (D) prefer to live with their friends

17. Which of the following can we infer from the passage?

    (A) Old people in China are increasing living on their own.

    (B) Things are easier than ever for young couples in China.

    (C) The typical Chinese family has remained unchanged for 10 years.

    (D) There is a housing shortage in some of the major cities in China.

Read this passage.

[Simplified-character version]	[Traditional-character version]
《论语》是一本伟大的书,它是孔子的学生编写的,记录了孔子说过的话和他日常生活的故事。《论语》中记载,孔子说过,为人正直坦率的朋友,对人宽容的朋友以及见多识广的朋友,这样的人都是好朋友。而脾气暴躁的朋友,做事犹豫不定的朋友,还有表面上对你热情,心里却在想坏主意的小人,这几种朋友是坏朋友。两千多年过去了,《论语》中提到的交友标准并没有过时。	《論語》是一本偉大的書,它是孔子的學生編寫的,記錄了孔子説過的話和他日常生活的故事。《論語》中記載,孔子説過,爲人正直坦率的朋友,對人寬容的朋友以及見多識廣的朋友,這樣的人都是好朋友。而脾氣暴躁的朋友,做事猶豫不定的朋友,還有表面上對你熱情,心裏卻在想壞主意的小人,這幾種朋友是壞朋友。兩千多年過去了,《論語》中提到的交友標準並沒有過時。

18. According to the passage, which of the following statements about the *Analects* is TRUE?

    (A) It is a great work written by Confucius.

    (B) It is a great work written by Confucius' teacher.

    (C) It is a record of what Confucius said and did in his lifetime.

    (D) It is a record of Chinese history during Confucius' time.

19. Which of the following statements is TRUE?

(A) The *Analects* mentions two types of good friends and two types of undesirable friends.

(B) The *Analects* mentions three types of good friends and three types of undesirable friends.

(C) The *Analects* mentions four types of good friends and three types of undesirable friends.

(D) The *Analects* mentions three types of good friends and four types of undesirable friends.

20. In this passage, what does "小人(小人)" mean?

(A) A hesitant person.

(B) A person with bad intentions.

(C) A miserly person.

(D) An bad-tempered person.

21. According to this passage, which statements about the measure of one's friends is TRUE?

(A) It is the central theme of the *Analects*.

(B) It can be interpreted differently in modern society.

(C) It was emphasized more strongly by Confucius' students than by Confucius himself.

(D) It can still be applied to people in modern society.

Read this public sign.

[Simplified-character version]   [Traditional-character version]

午睡时间请勿吵闹   午睡時間請勿吵鬧

22. Where would this sign most likely appear?

(A) In a library

(B) In a bookshop

(C) In a classroom

(D) In a student dormitory

23. What does this sign mean?

(A) No talking during exams.

(B) Please keep quiet in the hallways.

(C) Please do not speak loudly during nap time.

(D) No parties are allowed after midnight.

Read this public sign.

[Simplified-character version]   [Traditional-character version]

易碎物品, 小心轻放   易碎物品, 小心輕放

24. Where would this sign most likely appear?
    (A) On a box of computer accessories
    (B) On a box of chocolates
    (C) On a crate of wines
    (D) On a box of limited edition books

25. What is the purpose of this sign?
    (A) To tell people that these items are very light.
    (B) To tell people that these items contain alcohol.
    (C) To tell people that these items are very rare.
    (D) To tell people that these items are very fragile.

Section Two

I. Free Response (Writing)

Note: In this part, you may NOT move back and forth among questions.

Directions: You will be asked to write in Chinese in a variety of ways. In each case, you will be asked to write for a specific purpose and to a specific person. You should write in as complete and as culturally appropriate a manner as possible, taking into account the purpose and the person described.

1. Story Narration

The four pictures present a story. Imagine you are writing the story to a friend. Narrate a complete story as suggested by the pictures. Give your story a beginning, a middle, and an end.

2. Personal Letter

Write a letter to your friend telling him about an argument you have had with your parents. First, write about what happened, how you feel about it, and what you intend to do now. Then ask if he has had a similar experience, and ask for his advice.

3. E-Mail Response

Read this e-mail from a friend and then type a response.

| File　Edit　View　Insert　Format　Tools　Message　Help |
| New ┊ Send ┊ Foward ┊ |

[Simplified-character version]	[Traditional-character version]
发件人: 赵明 主　题: 关于美国家庭的一些问题	發件人: 趙明 主　題: 關於美國家庭的一些問題
我和同学最近要写一个关于中美家庭教育问题的调查报告。我们已经通过上网、在图书馆查文章和报刊消息等, 找到了我们想要的一些资料, 但是还不够。现在, 我们想请美国的朋友帮我们做一些简单的问题调查, 如果你愿意的话, 能不能告诉我: 1.你觉得对于美国家庭来说, 家庭教育最重视的是什么? 2.美国家庭中的父母通常最关注孩子哪方面的发展, 而且一般会提供哪些支持? 希望你能告诉我你对这些问题的想法, 并能举一些简单的例子说明一下。盼望尽快收到你的回信。谢谢!	我和同學最近要寫一個關於中美家庭教育問題的調查報告。我們已經通過上網、在圖書館查文章和報刊消息等, 找到了我們想要的一些資料, 但是還不夠。現在, 我們想請美國的朋友幫我們做一些簡單的問題調查, 如果你願意的話, 能不能告訴我: 1.你覺得對於美國家庭來說, 家庭教育最重視的是什麼? 2.美國家庭中的父母通常最關注孩子哪方面的發展, 而且一般會提供哪些支持? 希望你能告訴我你對這些問題的想法, 並能舉一些簡單的例子說明一下。盼望儘快收到你的回信。謝謝!

4. Relay a Telephone Message

Imagine your father is away on business and will be back tomorrow. You arrive home and listen to a message for him on the answering machine. However, you are about to leave for a trip and will only be back two days later. You will listen to the message twice. Then relay the message, including the important details, by typing a note to your father.

II. Free Response (Speaking)

Note: In this part, you may NOT move back and forth among questions.

Directions: You will participate in a simulated conversation. Each time it is your turn to speak, you will have 20 seconds to record. You should respond as completely and as appropriately as possible.

1. Conversation

You will have a conversation with Huang Xiaoli, a local TV reporter, about your views on the roles of parents.

Directions: You will be asked to speak in Chinese on different topics in the following two questions. In each case, imagine you are making an oral presentation to your class or your family in Chinese. First, you will read and hear the topic for your presentation. You will have 4 minutes to prepare your presentation. Then you will have 2 minutes to record your presentation. Your presentation should be as complete as possible.

2. Cultural Presentation

Choose ONE modern Chinese writer you know about or like. In your presentation, talk about the writer's work, and your opinion of their work. If possible, talk about what you know of this writer's upbringing and background.

3. Event Plan

Your family has the opportunity to plan a one-week homestay for a Chinese student. Your father has made some arrangements. In your presentation, give your opinion of your father's arrangements. Then, give your own recommendations and justify them.

UNIT FOUR
LESSON 7
Festivals and Customs
Celebrating Chinese New Year

Section One

I. Multiple Choice (Listen to the dialogs)

Note: In this part, you may NOT move back and forth among questions.

Directions: In this part, you will hear several short conversations or parts of conversations followed by four choices, designated (A), (B), (C), and (D). Choose the one that continues or completes the conversation in a logical and culturally appropriate manner. You will have 5 seconds to answer each question.

1.	(A)	(B)	(C)	(D)	5.	(A)	(B)	(C)	(D)
2.	(A)	(B)	(C)	(D)	6.	(A)	(B)	(C)	(D)
3.	(A)	(B)	(C)	(D)	7.	(A)	(B)	(C)	(D)
4.	(A)	(B)	(C)	(D)	8.	(A)	(B)	(C)	(D)

II. Multiple Choice (Listen to the selections)

Note: In this part, you may move back and forth only among the questions associated with the current listening selection.

Directions: In this part, you will listen to several selections in Chinese. For each selection, you will be told whether it will be played once or twice. You may take notes as you listen. After listening to each selection, you will see questions in English. For each question, choose the response that is best according to the selection. You will have 12 seconds to answer each question.

Selection 1

1. Which traditional Chinese festival did Xiao Li experience in China?
   - (A) The Lantern Festival
   - (B) The Dragon Boat Festival
   - (C) The Moon Festival
   - (D) Chinese New Year

2. Why was Xiao Li's friend's house bustling with activity?

    (A) Because many friends were there.

    (B) Because many relatives were there.

    (C) Because there had been an accident.

    (D) Because someone was playing with fire crackers.

3. According to the passage, which of the following statements is TRUE?

    (A) Xiao Li had rice dumplings at her friend's place.

    (B) Xiao Li received a red packet from her friend's mother.

    (C) Xiao Li enjoyed herself at her friend's place.

    (D) Xiao Li greeted her friend's father with best wishes.

Selection 2

4. According to the passage, what strange thing did Lily encounter?

    (A) Her school was closed for the day.

    (B) There were lots of decorations in the streets.

    (C) A local store was very crowded.

    (D) People were carrying colored lanterns.

5. How did Lily learn about the origin of the Lantern Festival?

    (A) Her friend told her about it.

    (B) A salesman told her about it.

    (C) She learned about it in class.

    (D) She had read about it in a book.

6. What does Lily intend to do now?

    (A) Eat rice dumplings at Xiao Wang's place.

    (B) Buy some rice dumplings for herself.

    (C) Find her teacher.

    (D) Go and buy a lantern.

Selection 3

7. When will the performance take place?

    (A) 9:30 pm this Friday

    (B) 9:30 pm next Friday

    (C) 7:30 pm next Friday

    (D) 7:30 pm this Friday

8. Where can a student register for the performance?

    (A) At the school broadcasting station

    (B) At the students' activity center

    (C) At the administrative office

    (D) At the school auditorium

9. What has yet to be decided about the performance?

    (A) Who the judges will be.

    (B) When the registration will begin.

    (C) Where it will be held.

    (D) How many participants there will be.

Selection 4

10. Which group of people celebrate the Songkran Festival?

    (A) The Bai people   (B) The Han people

    (C) The Dai people   (D) All ethnic communities in China

11. In which part of China is the Songkran Festival celebrated?

    (A) The Southeast   (B) The Southwest

    (C) The South   (D) The North

Selection 5

12. Why did the sports center adjust its operating hours?

    (A) Because students made a request to the management.

    (B) Because its equipment needed repairs.

    (C) Because of the public holidays during Chinese New Year.

    (D) Because a competition was being held.

13. Will the sports center open on the third day of the Chinese Lunar Year?

    (A) No, it will stay closed.

    (B) Yes, it will open as usual.

    (C) Yes, but the operating hours will be different from usual.

    (D) No, but the staff will be on call.

14. What are the usual operating hours of the sports center?

    (A) 10:00 am to 3:00 pm

    (B) 8:30 am to 3:00 pm

    (C) 8:30 am to 9:00 pm

    (D) 10:00 am to 5:00 pm

III. Multiple Choice (Reading)

Note: In this part, you may move back and forth among all the questions.

Directions: You will read several selections in Chinese. Each selection is accompanied by a number of questions in English. For each question, choose the response that is best according to the selection.

Read this passage.

[Simplified-character version]	[Traditional-character version]
玛丽在网上认识了一个中国朋友，他们偶尔也打打电话。有了这个中国朋友以后，玛丽对中国文化产生了很大的兴趣。玛丽听他说春节是中国人最重要的节日，为了祝贺朋友节日快乐，12月30号她给这位朋友寄去了一封电子邮件，第二天晚上，玛丽打开邮箱就看到了中国朋友的回信，信的内容是："你好! 也祝你新年快乐，你问我们今天过年有没有吃饺子，真的很抱歉，也许上次我没有说清楚，中国人的过年一般是指农历的正月初一，你的邮件说的是公历的日期。一般来说农历的日期比公历的日期晚一个月左右，今天是农历12月1号, 离过年还有一个月呢。小明"	瑪麗在網上認識了一個中國朋友，他們偶爾也打打電話。有了這個中國朋友以後，瑪麗對中國文化產生了很大的興趣。瑪麗聽他說春節是中國人最重要的節日，爲了祝賀朋友節日快樂，12月30號她給這位朋友寄去了一封電子郵件，第二天晚上，瑪麗打開郵箱就看到了中國朋友的回信，信的內容是："你好! 也祝你新年快樂，你問我們今天過年有沒有吃餃子，真的很抱歉，也許上次我沒有說清楚，中國人的過年一般是指農曆的正月初一，你的郵件說的是公曆的日期。一般來說農曆的日期比公曆的日期晚一個月左右，今天是農曆12月1號, 離過年還有一個月呢。小明"

1. How did Mary get to know her Chinese friend, Xiao Ming?
    (A) They met on holiday.
    (B) They met at a party.
    (C) They met through a mutual friend.
    (D) They met online.

2. Why did Mary send Xiao Ming an e-mail?
    (A) Because she wanted to know more about Chinese culture.
    (B) Because she wanted to know the differences between festive celebrations in China and in the United States.
    (C) Because she wanted to wish Xiao Ming a happy Chinese New Year.
    (D) Because she wanted to ask Xiao Ming how New Year is celebrated in China.

3. Which of the following statements is TRUE?

(A) Xiao Ming's family will eat dumplings on December 30.

(B) Solar dates always come after lunar dates.

(C) Mary received Xiao Ming's reply one day before New Year.

(D) Mary has always been interested in Chinese culture.

Read this note.

[Simplified-character version]

小星：
　　听说你昨天买了一个手机，正要买手机号码。学校操场的南边有一家商店，那儿的卡号挺多的，而且也实惠，你可以去那儿瞧瞧，用不着去正式的手机营业大厅了。那家商店里的手机号价格不一样，一般来说，包含数字4的号码会多一些，并且也便宜一点；包含数字8的号码少一点，而且也会贵一些。看来，大家都喜欢8，而不太喜欢4。不过总的来说那儿的号码都不算贵，价钱在50~100元左右。

小红
7月9日

[Traditional-character version]

小星：
　　聽說你昨天買了一個手機，正要買手機號碼。學校操場的南邊有一家商店，那兒的卡號挺多的，而且也實惠，你可以去那兒瞧瞧，用不著去正式的手機營業大廳了。那家商店裏的手機號價格不一樣，一般來說，包含數字4的號碼會多一些，並且也便宜一點；包含數字8的號碼少一點，而且也會貴一些。看來，大家都喜歡8，而不太喜歡4。不過總的來說那兒的號碼都不算貴，價錢在50~100元左右。

小紅
7月9日

4. What does Xiao Hong say about the shop at the south of the sports ground?

(A) The cell phone numbers available there are good.

(B) The prices of cell phone numbers there are reasonable.

(C) The cost of a new cell phone number can be as little as 40 *yuan*.

(D) The shop has more cell phone numbers with 8 than with 4.

5. Which of the following is mentioned in the note?

    (A) The shop where Xiao Xing bought his new cell phone.

    (B) The functions of Xiao Xing's new cell phone.

    (C) The price range of cell phone numbers.

    (D) The reasons why people prefer the number 8 to the number 4.

Read this notice.

[Simplified-character version]	[Traditional-character version]
新春的脚步越来越近了, 蜜蜂书友会也将陪伴着会员们迈进旺旺的狗年! 为了感谢会员们对蜜蜂书友会一年来的支持和厚爱, 大年初四上午10:30我们将举办"蜜蜂新春知识竞赛"。请所有热爱书的"蜜蜂"们一起来过年! 活动内容: 关于中国春节及过年风俗的 知识抢答赛 活动时间: 2月1日大年初四 上午10:30 活动地点: 蜜蜂书友会西城中心 广宁路550号D座 报名方式: 拨打蜜蜂书友会热线 64474137 / 64474132 或点击**此处**直接留下您的姓名、年龄、电话, 以及您将表演的节目。 本次活动免费, 蜜蜂书友会会员优先!	新春的脚步越來越近了, 蜜蜂書友會也將陪伴著會員們邁進旺旺的狗年! 爲了感謝會員們對蜜蜂書友會一年來的支持和厚愛, 大年初四上午10:30我們將舉辦"蜜蜂新春知識競賽"。請所有熱愛書的"蜜蜂"們一起來過年! 活動內容: 關於中國春節及過年風俗的 知識搶答賽 活動時間: 2月1日大年初四 上午10:30 活動地點: 蜜蜂書友會西城中心 廣寧路550號D座 報名方式: 撥打蜜蜂書友會熱綫 64474137 / 64474132 或點擊**此處**直接留下您的姓名、年齡、電話, 以及您將表演的節目。 本次活動免費, 蜜蜂書友會會員優先!

6. From this notice, we can infer that _____ .

    (A) members of this book club have priority to participate in this activity

    (B) interested people can go to Block D, No. 550 Guangning Road to register

    (C) the Lantern Festival is on February 10

    (D) this year is the Year of the Dog

7. Which of the following questions will be tested in the Q&A contest?

(A) What do people usually do during the Moon Festival?

(B) What is the purpose of having rice dumplings and dragon boat racing?

(C) Why must children stay awake on the eve of Chinese New Year until midnight?

(D) Why is "Qi Xi" known as Chinese Valentines' Day?

Read this passage.

[Simplified-character version]	[Traditional-character version]
农历十二月八日，又叫腊八，传说这一天是佛祖释迦牟尼得道的日子。后来人们为了纪念他，在这一天都吃腊八粥。腊八粥的做法是用大米和红枣、红豆、花生、葡萄等一起煮，有的人家甚至能加入二十余种材料。腊八粥从腊月初七晚上一直熬到第二天的清晨。熬好以后，要先祭祀祖先，然后在中午以前送给亲朋好友，最后才是全家人自己吃。一般来说，各家煮的腊八粥都很多，往往能吃上好几天，因为人们认为腊八粥多得吃不完，是表示年年有余的意思。	農曆十二月八日，又叫臘八，傳說這一天是佛祖釋迦牟尼得道的日子。後來人們爲了紀念他，在這一天都吃臘八粥。臘八粥的做法是用大米和紅棗、紅豆、花生、葡萄等一起煮，有的人家甚至能加入二十餘種材料。臘八粥從臘月初七晚上一直熬到第二天的清晨。熬好以後，要先祭祀祖先，然後在中午以前送給親朋好友，最後才是全家人自己吃。一般來說，各家煮的臘八粥都很多，往往能吃上好幾天，因爲人們認爲臘八粥多得吃不完，是表示年年有餘的意思。

8. Which of the following statements about Laba Porridge is TRUE?

(A) It should be served to family members first, then relatives.

(B) It has at least 20 kinds of ingredients.

(C) It needs to be boiled overnight.

(D) It must be finished within two days.

9. Why do people usually cook lots of Laba Porridge?

(A) Because the amount of porridge you cook represents a family's wealth.

(B) Because they usually to share it with friends and relatives.

(C) Because they want to eat it for several days.

(D) Because having lots of leftovers is significant.

Read this passage.

[Simplified-character version]	[Traditional-character version]
我对童年的记忆已经比较模糊，不过有几件事我却记得很清楚。第一是我对飞机和大船有一种天生的好感，而且从小就知道，这个世界比我所想象的还要大得多。九岁的时候，我第一次坐飞机，一点也不害怕，一直想着飞机为什么没有我想象中的那样飞得很高很高。第二是我爸爸很喜欢看电影，常常吃完晚饭，就带着我看晚上七点的电影。电影五块钱一场，非常便宜。从那个时候起，我就对电影产生了深厚的感情，打算高中毕业以后，到美国学电影专业。	我對童年的記憶已經比較模糊，不過有幾件事我卻記得很清楚。第一是我對飛機和大船有一種天生的好感，而且從小就知道，這個世界比我所想像的還要大得多。九歲的時候，我第一次坐飛機，一點也不害怕，一直想著飛機爲什麽沒有我想像中的那樣飛得很高很高。第二是我爸爸很喜歡看電影，常常吃完晚飯，就帶著我看晚上七點的電影。電影五塊錢一場，非常便宜。從那個時候起，我就對電影產生了深厚的感情，打算高中畢業以後，到美國學電影專業。

10. What is the article about?

    (A) It is about the author's future plans.

    (B) It is about the author's growing pains.

    (C) It is about the author's memories of his childhood.

    (D) It is about the author's memories of his father.

11. When the author was young, what did he used to do?

    (A) He used to travel a lot.

    (B) He used to eat a lot.

    (C) He used to go to the movies very often.

    (D) He used to play sports very often.

12. According to the passage, which of the following statements is TRUE?

    (A) The author intends to pursue film studies in the United States.

    (B) It used to be very expensive to watch movies.

    (C) The author took his first flight when he was eight years old.

    (D) The author felt scared when he flew for the first time.

Read this notice.

[Simplified-character version]	[Traditional-character version]
一年一度的重阳老人节即将来临,为了庆祝这个传统的节日,学校9月27日(农历九月初九,重阳节)将组织同学们去爬山,同时也欢迎各位同学的爷爷奶奶参加活动。 　　以下是活动的具体安排: 9:00　　学校东门口集合 9:20　　爬山比赛 11:00　　登高赏菊 12:00　　午餐,喝菊花茶,吃重阳糕 1:30　　同学们给爷爷奶奶们送礼物 3:30　　爷爷奶奶们讲话 4:00　　活动结束 　　请各班班长统计好参加活动的人数(包括同学们的爷爷奶奶),在9月25日以前交到学生会办公室。 　　提前祝各位同学的爷爷奶奶重阳节快乐! 　　　　　　　　　　校学生会 　　　　　　　　　　9月20日	一年一度的重陽老人節即將來臨,爲了慶祝這個傳統的節日,學校9月27日(農曆九月初九,重陽節)將組織同學們去爬山,同時也歡迎各位同學的爺爺奶奶參加活動。 　　以下是活動的具體安排: 9:00　　學校東門口集合 9:20　　爬山比賽 11:00　　登高賞菊 12:00　　午餐,喝菊花茶,吃重陽糕 1:30　　同學們給爺爺奶奶們送禮物 3:30　　爺爺奶奶們講話 4:00　　活動結束 　　請各班班長統計好參加活動的人數(包括同學們的爺爺奶奶),在9月25日以前交到學生會辦公室。 　　提前祝各位同學的爺爺奶奶重陽節快樂! 　　　　　　　　　　校學生會 　　　　　　　　　　9月20日

13. When is Elderly Festival held?

   (A) On the ninth day of the ninth month of the Chinese lunar calendar.

   (B) On the twenty-seventh day of the ninth month of the Chinese lunar calendar.

   (C) On September 20 of the solar calendar.

   (D) On September 9 of the solar calendar.

14. Which of the following can the participants expect on that day?

   (A) A great view of the sunset.

   (B) The chance to take part in traditional games.

   (C) Mountain climbing.

   (D) The chance to view *mei* blossoms.

15. What do students need to prepare in advance?

   (A) They need to bring chrysanthemum tea leaves to the hilltop.

   (B) They need to prepare a performance to entertain their grandparents.

   (C) They need to bring their own lunchboxes.

   (D) They need to prepare a small gift for their grandparents.

Read this letter.

[Simplified-character version]	[Traditional-character version]

爸爸：
 	
    上个星期天我和朋友小李一起参加了他哥哥的婚礼。那天上午，好几辆贴有"囍"字的汽车从小李家门口开走了，听小李说，是他哥哥去新娘子家接新娘子了。十一点左右，他哥哥和新娘子回来了，新娘子穿了一身红色的衣服，非常漂亮。中午十二点整，我们一起吃饭，来的客人很多，足足有二十来桌。新郎和新娘可忙坏了，得一桌一桌地发喜糖，还有很多人跟他哥哥和新娘子开玩笑。下午我们去参观了他哥哥的新房，房间布置得很漂亮，房间里的衣柜上、窗户上到处都贴上了"囍"字。参观完他哥哥的房间，我们才离开。我觉得这真是非常愉快的一天！
 	
                  儿子
              5月2日
	爸爸：
	
	    上個星期天我和朋友小李一起參加了他哥哥的婚禮。那天上午，好幾輛貼有"囍"字的汽車從小李家門口開走了，聽小李說，是他哥哥去新娘子家接新娘子了。十一點左右，他哥哥和新娘子回來了，新娘子穿了一身紅色的衣服，非常漂亮。中午十二點整，我們一起吃飯，來的客人很多，足足有二十來桌。新郎和新娘可忙壞了，得一桌一桌地發喜糖，還有很多人跟他哥哥和新娘子開玩笑。下午我們去參觀了他哥哥的新房，房間布置得很漂亮，房間裏的衣櫃上、窗戶上到處都貼上了"囍"字。參觀完他哥哥的房間，我們才離開。我覺得這真是非常愉快的一天！
	
	                  兒子
	              5月2日

16. Where did the cars go to in the morning?

   (A) They were driven to the bride's house.

   (B) They were driven to Xiao Li's parents' house.

   (C) They were driven to a restaurant.

   (D) They were driven to Xiao Li's brother's new house.

17. Why were Xiao Li's brother and his wife so busy?

   (A) Because the guests kept talking to them.

   (B) Because there were too many guests.

   (C) Because they were busy decorating their home.

   (D) Because they needed to take photographs with every guest.

18. Which of the following statements is TRUE?

    (A) The bride wore a beautiful white wedding gown.

    (B) The author visited the wedding room that afternoon.

    (C) Xiao Li's brother and the bride did not hand out wedding sweets.

    (D) The author stayed at Xiao Li's brother's place for the whole day.

Read this public sign.

[Simplified-character version]

欢度佳节

[Traditional-character version]

歡度佳節

19. When do people usually hang this sign up?

    (A) During special occasions

    (B) During meetings

    (C) During certain festivals

    (D) On someone's birthday

20. What is the function of this sign?

    (A) To let people know about a sale.

    (B) To advertise a new product.

    (C) To direct traffic.

    (D) To urge people to enjoy themselves.

Read this sentence.

[Simplified-character version]

燕子飞得低,出门带雨衣。

[Traditional-character version]

燕子飛得低,出門帶雨衣。

21. When do people usually say the sentence above?

    (A) Before it rains.

    (B) Before a snowfall.

    (C) On sunny days.

    (D) On windy days.

Section Two

Note: In this part, you may NOT move back and forth among questions.

I. Free Response (Writing)

Directions: You will be asked to write in Chinese in a variety of ways. In each case, you will be asked to write for a specific purpose and to a specific person. You should write in as complete and as culturally appropriate a manner as possible, taking into account the purpose and the person described.

1. Story Narration

The four pictures present a story. Imagine you are writing the story to a friend. Narrate a complete story as suggested by the pictures. Give your story a beginning, a middle, and an end.

2. Personal Letter

Imagine you received a latter from a pen pal. The letter talks about how people celebrate Chinese New Year these days as compared to in the past. Your pen pal says he misses celebrating Chinese New Year at his grandparents' village as a child. He also asks how you celebrate New Year in the United States, how New Year customs have changed over the years, and your opinions on these changes. Write a reply in letter format to discuss these issues.

3. E-Mail Response

Read this e-mail from a friend and then type a response.

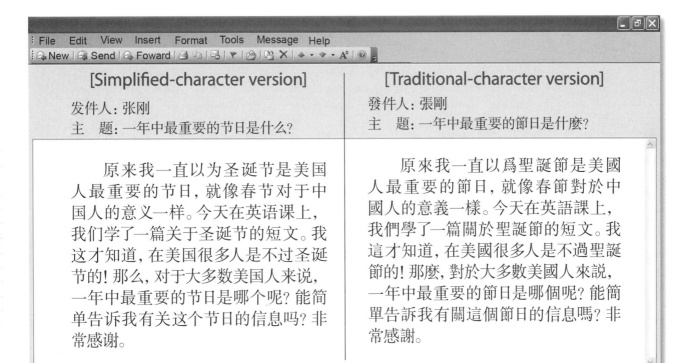

| File | Edit | View | Insert | Format | Tools | Message | Help |

New | Send | Foward |

[Simplified-character version]

发件人: 张刚
主　题: 一年中最重要的节日是什么?

　　原来我一直以为圣诞节是美国人最重要的节日, 就像春节对于中国人的意义一样。今天在英语课上, 我们学了一篇关于圣诞节的短文。我这才知道, 在美国很多人是不过圣诞节的! 那么, 对于大多数美国人来说, 一年中最重要的节日是哪个呢? 能简单告诉我有关这个节日的信息吗? 非常感谢。

[Traditional-character version]

發件人: 張剛
主　題: 一年中最重要的節日是什麼?

　　原來我一直以爲聖誕節是美國人最重要的節日, 就像春節對於中國人的意義一樣。今天在英語課上, 我們學了一篇關於聖誕節的短文。我這才知道, 在美國很多人是不過聖誕節的! 那麼, 對於大多數美國人來説, 一年中最重要的節日是哪個呢? 能簡單告訴我有關這個節日的信息嗎? 非常感謝。

4. Relay a Telephone Message

Imagine you are working part time in a Chinese restaurant. You arrive one day and listen to a message for your manager on the answering machine. The message is from one of his friends who wants to reserve a table. You will listen to the message twice. Then relay the message, including the important details, by typing a note to your manager.

II. Free Response (Speaking)

Note: In this part, you may NOT move back and forth among questions.

Directions: You will participate in a simulated conversation. Each time it is your turn to speak, you will have 20 seconds to record. You should respond as fully and as appropriately as possible.

1. Conversation

A student of a partner school in China is studying the same topic as you. You will have a conversation with her about festivals in the United States.

Directions: You will be asked to speak in Chinese on different topics in the following two questions. In each case, imagine you are making an oral presentation to your class in Chinese. First, you will read and hear the topic for your presentation. You will have 4 minutes to prepare your presentation. Then you will have 2 minutes to record your presentation. Your presentation should be as complete as possible.

2. Cultural Presentation

In your presentation, talk about how Chinese people celebrate Chinese New Year.

3. Event Plan

Chinese New Year is around the corner. You and your best friends are planning to have a Chinese New Year party. In your presentation, describe your plan to your classmates and compare it with other plans. Talk about why you think this would be a good way to celebrate Chinese New Year.

UNIT FOUR
LESSON 8 · Festivals and Customs
Moon Festival

Section One

I. Multiple Choice (Listen to the dialogs)

Note: In this part, you may NOT move back and forth among questions.

Directions: In this part, you will hear several short conversations or parts of conversations followed by four choices, designated (A), (B), (C), and (D). Choose the one that continues or completes the conversation in a logical and culturally appropriate manner. You will have 5 seconds to answer each question.

1.	(A)	(B)	(C)	(D)		5.	(A)	(B)	(C)	(D)
2.	(A)	(B)	(C)	(D)		6.	(A)	(B)	(C)	(D)
3.	(A)	(B)	(C)	(D)		7.	(A)	(B)	(C)	(D)
4.	(A)	(B)	(C)	(D)		8.	(A)	(B)	(C)	(D)

II. Multiple Choice (Listen to the selections)

Note: In this part, you may move back and forth only among the questions associated with the current listening selection.

Directions: In this part, you will listen to several selections in Chinese. For each selection, you will be told whether it will be played once or twice. You may take notes as you listen. After listening to each selection, you will see questions in English. For each question, choose the response that is best according to the selection. You will have 12 seconds to answer each question.

Selection 1

1. What did Jack tell his mother?
   (A) He was going to visit a historical building.
   (B) Many of his classmates are local people.
   (C) He visited a classmate in Beijing.
   (D) He liked staying with his friends.

2. What kind of family can be called "四世同堂（四世同堂）"?

   (A) A family with four generations living together.

   (B) A family living in a four-bedroom apartment.

   (C) A family with four or more children.

   (D) A family in which both sets of grandparents live together.

3. How many people are there in Jack's classmate's family?

   (A) Four

   (B) Five

   (C) Six

   (D) Seven

Selection 2

4. Why does the woman mention the dragon boat race?

   (A) She is listening to a radio program about traditional festivals.

   (B) She is watching a dragon boat race on the TV.

   (C) She is reading a special report on the Dragon Boat Festival in the newspaper.

   (D) She is looking at a poster about the Dragon Boat Festival.

5. Why are the boats called "dragon boat"?

   (A) Because the dragon is a symbol of the Chinese people.

   (B) Because people believe that the dragon is the king of the sea.

   (C) Because ancient people believed that dragons move very quickly.

   (D) Because the boats are decorated to look like legendary dragons.

6. From the conversation, which of the following statements is TRUE?

   (A) Traditionally, *Zongzi* is wrapped with bamboo leaves.

   (B) A dragon boat race is held on May 5 every year.

   (C) People usually eat pyramid-shaped dumplings during the Dragon Boat Festival.

   (D) The Dragon Boat Festival is held in honor of a poet whose family name is *Lóng* (Dragon).

Selection 3

7. What did the woman find interesting about the man's clothes?

   (A) They were very inappropriate for the occasion.

   (B) They did not fit him very well.

   (C) They were very colorful.

   (D) They were very traditional.

8. When did the man buy his clothes?
    (A) Last weekend
    (B) Last February
    (C) During the winter vacation last year
    (D) During Chinese New Year last year

9. What are the two people going to do later?
    (A) They are going to watch a Chinese movie.
    (B) They are going to buy a suit.
    (C) They are going to shop for a birthday present.
    (D) They are going to a friend's party.

Selection 4

10. Why does the man say that the temperature will drop tonight?
    (A) Because it will be windy.
    (B) Because it will rain.
    (C) Because it will snow.
    (D) Because of freak weather conditions.

11. What will the highest temperature be tomorrow?
    (A) -1°C
    (B) 1°C
    (C) 5°C
    (D) 10°C

12. According to the message, when will the weather clear up?
    (A) Tomorrow morning
    (B) Tomorrow afternoon
    (C) Tomorrow evening
    (D) Tomorrow night

III. Multiple Choice (Reading)

Note: In this part, you may move back and forth among all the questions.

Directions: You will read several selections in Chinese. Each selection is accompanied by a number of questions in English. For each question, choose the response that is best according to the selection.

Read this poster.

[Simplified-character version]

最新娱乐信息

演出内容	地点	演出时间	票价	售票情况
新年音乐会	北京体育场	1月3日，19:30	¥180.00	已售完
东方歌舞团新春歌舞表演	北京展览馆剧场	2月11日，20:00	¥280.00	未售完
邓丽君经典歌曲演唱会	北京音乐厅	1月4日至1月9日，共五场。每天晚上18:30开演。	¥80.00	已售完
超级红星校园演唱会	北京大学五四操场	2月10日，19:00	¥120.00 ¥70.00	未售完

欢迎订票!
订票电话: 010–54901179。市内免费送票上门, 票到付款。
地址: 北京市朝阳区南路街18号欢乐票务公司　　邮编: 100080

[Traditional-character version]

最新娛樂信息

演出內容	地點	演出時間	票價	售票情況
新年音樂會	北京體育場	1月3日，19:30	¥180.00	已售完
東方歌舞團新春歌舞表演	北京展覽館劇場	2月11日，20:00	¥280.00	未售完
鄧麗君經典歌曲演唱會	北京音樂廳	1月4日至1月9日，共五場。每天晚上18:30開演。	¥80.00	已售完
超級紅星校園演唱會	北京大學五四操場	2月10日，19:00	¥120.00 ¥70.00	未售完

歡迎訂票!
訂票電話: 010–54901179。市內免費送票上門, 票到付款。
地址: 北京市朝陽區南路街18號歡樂票務公司　　郵編: 100080

1. A man has only 100 *yuan*. Which concert can he still buy tickets for?

    (A) The New Year concert

    (B) The New Oriental Song & Dance Troupe's New Year performance

    (C) The Deng Lijun's Classic Songs concert

    (D) The Super Stars' campus concert

2. If a person wants to watch performances at a stadium, which performance can he go to?

    (A) The New Year concert

    (B) The New Oriental Song & Dance Troupe's New Year performance

    (C) The Deng Lijun's Classic Songs concert

    (D) The Super Stars' campus concert

3. If someone requests the ticket to be delivered, how can he pay for it?

    (A) He can pay with a credit card.

    (B) He can pay in cash upon receipt of the ticket.

    (C) He can pay online.

    (D) He can mail a check to the ticketing company.

Read this passage.

[Simplified-character version]	[Traditional-character version]
中国有56个民族，每个民族过春节的方式不完全相同。比如：除夕那天，藏族人要举行盛大的晚会，大家在一起唱歌跳舞，庆祝新年的到来。到了新年早晨，藏族人要去外面挑水，新年挑的水是"吉祥水"，预祝新的一年吉祥如意。彝族人在快过年的时候，会在门前种一棵松树，希望来年平平安安。大年初一早晨，彝族人起床的第一件事就是挑水回家，他们会把新挑来的水和原来的水比一比，如果新挑来的水重，就代表今年雨水充足，收成会很好。	中國有56個民族，每個民族過春節的方式不完全相同。比如：除夕那天，藏族人要舉行盛大的晚會，大家在一起唱歌跳舞，慶祝新年的到來。到了新年早晨，藏族人要去外面挑水，新年挑的水是"吉祥水"，預祝新的一年吉祥如意。彝族人在快過年的時候，會在門前種一棵松樹，希望來年平平安安。大年初一早晨，彝族人起床的第一件事就是挑水回家，他們會把新挑來的水和原來的水比一比，如果新挑來的水重，就代表今年雨水充足，收成會很好。

4. According to the passage, the differences between the way Tibetans and the Yi people celebrate Chinese New Year are:

    (A) Tibetans uses pine leaves and pine cones to decorate their homes, while Yi people don't.

    (B) Tibetans dance on the morning of Chinese New Year, while the Yi people don't.

    (C) The Yi people have a party on the eve of Chinese New Year, while Tibetans don't.

    (D) The Yi people plant pine trees in front of their doors, while Tibetans don't.

5. According to the passage, why do Tibetans carry water into their houses during Chinese New Year?

    (A) To pray for a smooth and lucky year.

    (B) To pray for more rain.

    (C) To pray for more wealth.

    (D) To pray for the safety of their family members throughout the year.

6. According to the passage, the Yi people compare the weight of this year's water with last year's in order to predict if _____ .

    (A) they will have a safe and lucky year

    (B) the rainy season will be longer or shorter

    (C) it is safe to hold certain ceremonies in the year

    (D) this year will have favorable weather

Read this passage.

[Simplified-character version]	[Traditional-character version]
我最爱家乡杭州的中秋节。记得那时候的中秋之夜，一家老小吃完晚饭后，就会围坐在桌边，一边赏月，一边吃月饼，大人们谈着家常，孩子们不停地欢笑，简直是人生的一大享受。现在人在国外，每到中秋，思乡的心情尤其强烈，往往要提前几天买几张电话卡，不停地往国内打电话，向亲人、朋友和邻居们问好。如今，中秋的月亮依然可以欣赏到，但是尝到的月饼总不及小时候的香了。	我最愛家鄉杭州的中秋節。記得那時候的中秋之夜，一家老小吃完晚飯後，就會圍坐在桌邊，一邊賞月，一邊吃月餅，大人們談著家常，孩子們不停地歡笑，簡直是人生的一大享受。現在人在國外，每到中秋，思鄉的心情尤其強烈，往往要提前幾天買幾張電話卡，不停地往國內打電話，向親人、朋友和鄰居們問好。如今，中秋的月亮依然可以欣賞到，但是嚐到的月餅總不及小時候的香了。

7. How does the author usually spend the Moon Festival these days?

    (A) She goes out with friends for dinner.

    (B) She calls home to chat with her family and relatives.

    (C) She buys moon cakes and shares them with neighbors.

    (D) She invites friends over to eat moon cakes while enjoying the view of the moon.

8. Why does the author say she will never be able to eat moon cake as delicious as those she used to eat in her childhood?

    (A) Because moon cakes are all made by machines these days.

    (B) Because the moon cakes she buys now are not made by her mother.

    (C) Because her feelings towards eating moon cakes has changed.

    (D) Because she doesn't really like moon cakes any more.

9. From the passage, we can infer that _____ .

    (A) the author prefers handmade moon cakes

    (B) the author used to spend the Moon Festival with friends

    (C) the author often goes back to China to visit her family

    (D) the author came from Hangzhou in China

Read this passage.

[Simplified-character version]	[Traditional-character version]
春节到了, 无论如何也要回家和亲人团聚, 这是中国人的传统。每年春节期间, 大量打工族、学生、探亲人群几乎在同一时间返回自己的家乡, 这时, 航空、铁路、公路运输会异常繁忙, 形成了独特的"春运现象"。多数人——特别是长途旅客——更愿意选择乘坐火车, 因为火车票价便宜, 又比较安全。但是春节坐火车回家实在是太挤了。2006年底, 铁道部部长表示, 中国铁路运输能力最近几年将会大幅度地提升, 希望在五年以后, "春运"期间繁忙、紧张的景象会成为历史。	春節到了, 無論如何也要回家和親人團聚, 這是中國人的傳統。每年春節期間, 大量打工族、學生、探親人群幾乎在同一時間返回自己的家鄉, 這時, 航空、鐵路、公路運輸會異常繁忙, 形成了獨特的"春運現象"。多數人——特別是長途旅客——更願意選擇乘坐火車, 因爲火車票價便宜, 又比較安全。但是春節坐火車回家實在是太擠了。2006年底, 鐵道部部長表示, 中國鐵路運輸能力最近幾年將會大幅度地提升, 希望在五年以後, "春運"期間繁忙、緊張的景象會成爲歷史。

10. Which of the following is mentioned in the passage?

(A) The price increase in train and bus tickets during Chinese New Year.

(B) The reasons behind the increase in traffic during Chinese New Year.

(C) Statistics about popular modes of transport during Chinese New Year.

(D) Solutions to traffic jams during Chinese New Year.

11. According to the passage, why do people choose to take the train when they travel during Chinese New Year?

(A) Because trains are usually safer than other modes of transport.

(B) Because the roads are very jammed during the period.

(C) Because trains are less crowded than buses.

(D) Because trains are more comfortable and faster than buses.

12. According to the passage, when will the traffic problem during Chinese New Year be solved?

(A) 2008   (B) 2009

(C) 2010   (D) 2011

13. "春运 (春運)"is an abbreviation, meaning _____ .

(A) 春天的运输系统(春天的運輸系統)。   (B) 春节期间的交通运输(春節期間的交通運輸)。

(C) 春天的运输问题(春天的運輸問題)。   (D) 春节期间的运输工程(春節期間的運輸工程)。

Read this note.

[Simplified-character version]	[Traditional-character version]
星星： 　　你的病怎么样了? 现在好些了吗? 再过一个星期就是教师节了, 我们全班同学今天开了个会, 决定教师节那天送老师一份特别的礼物: 每位同学提供一张自己的电子照片, 再加上全班的集体照, 然后配上音乐, 做成一张光盘。因此, 请将你的照片发到我们班的邮箱: tofor@163.com。另外, 别忘了在照片旁写上你给老师的祝福。光盘做好后, 我们会通知你的, 放心吧。 　　　祝 早日康复! 　　　　　　　　　　　　小华 　　　　　　　　　　　　9月3日	星星： 　　你的病怎麼樣了? 現在好些了嗎? 再過一個星期就是教師節了, 我們全班同學今天開了個會, 決定教師節那天送老師一份特別的禮物: 每位同學提供一張自己的電子照片, 再加上全班的集體照, 然後配上音樂, 做成一張光盤。因此, 請將你的照片發到我們班的郵箱: tofor@163.com。另外, 別忘了在照片旁寫上你給老師的祝福。光盤做好後, 我們會通知你的, 放心吧。 　　　祝 早日康復! 　　　　　　　　　　　　小華 　　　　　　　　　　　　9月3日

14. What does "早日康复（早日康復）" mean?

    (A) Have a nice day!

    (B) Have a good journey!

    (C) Get well soon!

    (D) Looking forward to hearing from you!

15. What will the students give to their teacher?

    (A) A photo album containing photos of every student.

    (B) A card signed by every student.

    (C) A CD containing the teacher's favorite music.

    (D) A CD-ROM containing photos and music.

16. According to the note, which of the following statements is TRUE?

    (A) Each student will need to write a letter to their teacher.

    (B) Xingxing needs to provide his photo and a short message.

    (C) Xingxing must e-mail Xiaohua by tomorrow.

    (D) Xiaohua is in charge of preparing the teacher's present.

Read this passage.

[Simplified-character version]	[Traditional-character version]
中国人一般认为，女孩到了三十岁就该有自己的家庭了。如果这时还没有自己的家庭，父母就会着急了：怎么还没有结婚呀？张红现在就遇到了这样的问题。父母总是希望她早点结婚，可张红又有什么办法呢？她曾经有过男朋友，但最后还是没有走到一起。后来她想通过网络认识新朋友，又觉得不太可靠。张红想不出别的办法了。现在，她的父母已经跟别人联系好，明天让她跟一个陌生的男人见面。张红整夜都没睡着觉，她真的不愿意通过这样的方式交男朋友。可是她想了想自己身边的很多朋友，他们不也是通过这种方式最后找到了自己的另一半吗？这种传统的方式又有什么不好呢？于是她决定明天去试一试。	中國人一般認爲，女孩到了三十歲就該有自己的家庭了。如果這時還沒有自己的家庭，父母就會著急了：怎麼還沒有結婚呀？張紅現在就遇到了這樣的問題。父母總是希望她早點結婚，可張紅又有什麼辦法呢？她曾經有過男朋友，但最後還是沒有走到一起。後來她想通過網絡認識新朋友，又覺得不太可靠。張紅想不出別的辦法了。現在，她的父母已經跟別人聯繫好，明天讓她跟一個陌生的男人見面。張紅整夜都沒睡著覺，她真的不願意通過這樣的方式交男朋友。可是她想了想自己身邊的很多朋友，他們不也是通過這種方式最後找到了自己的另一半嗎？這種傳統的方式又有什麼不好呢？於是她決定明天去試一試。

17. What problem is Zhang Hong facing?

    (A) She often works late and has no time to socialize.

    (B) She is having trouble sleeping.

    (C) She is always arguing with her parents.

    (D) She is almost thirty but still single.

18. What does "最后没有走到一起（最后没有走到一起）" mean?

    (A) They didn't walk at the same speed.

    (B) They followed different career paths.

    (C) They didn't get married.

    (D) They got a divorce.

19. What does Zhang Hong think about blind dates?

    (A) They are worth trying since they can sometimes work out.

    (B) She is fine with them as she doesn't want to disappoint her parents.

    (C) She worries that people may laugh at her.

    (D) She feels uncomfortable meeting strangers.

20. According to the passage, which of the following statements is TRUE?

    (A) Zhang Hong has never had a boyfriend before.

    (B) Many of Zhang Hong's friends met their partners through blind dates.

    (C) Zhang Hong intends to find a boyfriend online.

    (D) Zhang Hong's parents arranged a blind date for her last week.

Read this phrase.

[Simplified-character version]   [Traditional-character version]

步步高升   步步高升

21. Where would this phrase most likely appear?

    (A) In a lift

    (B) In an office

    (C) On a greeting card

    (D) On the side of a bus

22. What is the function of this phrase?

    (A) To remind people to smile.

    (B) To encourage people to keep working hard.

    (C) To offer good wishes for one's career.

    (D) To advertize a product.

Read this public sign.

[Simplified-character version]

高高兴兴上班去, 平平安安回家来。

[Traditional-character version]

高高興興上班去, 平平安安回家來。

23. Where would this sign most likely appear?

(A) In an office

(B) In a residential area

(C) In a shopping mall

(D) At a construction site

24. What is the purpose of this sign?

(A) To wish everyone a pleasant journey to and from work.

(B) To warn people of possible danger in the area.

(C) To remind people to be wary of pickpockets.

(D) To encourage people to come to work and go home on time.

Section Two

I. Free Response (Writing)

Note: In this part, you may NOT move back and forth among questions.

Directions: You will be asked to write in Chinese in a variety of ways. In each case, you will be asked to write for a specific purpose and to a specific person. You should write in as complete and as culturally appropriate a manner as possible, taking into account the purpose and the person described.

1. Story Narration

The four pictures present a story. Imagine you are writing the story to a friend. Narrate a complete story as suggested by the pictures. Give your story a beginning, a middle, and an end.

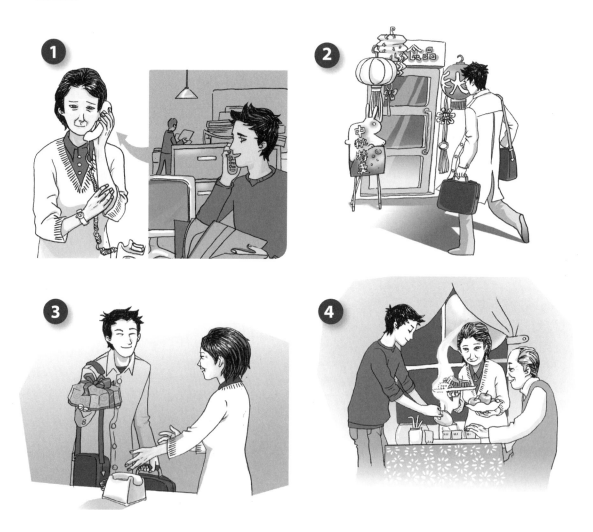

2. Personal Letter

Imagine you received a letter from a pen pal. In the letter, he mentions that young people in China like to celebrate western festivals, among which Valentine's Day is the most popular. However, he knows nothing about this festival and would like to find out more from you. Write a reply in letter format. Tell your pen pal about the origins of Valentine's Day and how it is celebrated in the United States. Provide as much detail as you can.

3. E-Mail Response

Read this e-mail from a friend and then type a response.

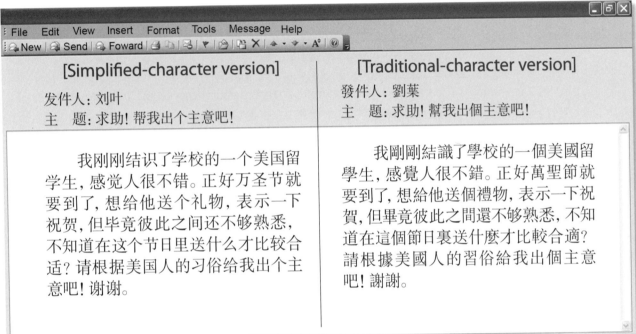

| File | Edit | View | Insert | Format | Tools | Message | Help |

New | Send | Foward |

[Simplified-character version]	[Traditional-character version]
发件人: 刘叶 主　题: 求助! 帮我出个主意吧!	發件人: 劉葉 主　題: 求助! 幫我出個主意吧!
我刚刚结识了学校的一个美国留学生, 感觉人很不错。正好万圣节就要到了, 想给他送个礼物, 表示一下祝贺, 但毕竟彼此之间还不够熟悉, 不知道在这个节日里送什么才比较合适? 请根据美国人的习俗给我出个主意吧! 谢谢。	我剛剛結識了學校的一個美國留學生, 感覺人很不錯。正好萬聖節就要到了, 想給他送個禮物, 表示一下祝賀, 但畢竟彼此之間還不夠熟悉, 不知道在這個節日裏送什麼才比較合適? 請根據美國人的習俗給我出個主意吧! 謝謝。

4. Relay a Telephone Message

Imagine your grandfather is visiting your family from China. You arrive home one day and listen to a message from your grandfather on the answering machine. The message is for your father. You will listen twice to the message. Then relay the message, including the important details, by typing a note to your father.

II. Free Response (Speaking)

Note: In this part, you may NOT move back and forth among questions.

Directions: You will participate in a simulated conversation. Each time it is your turn to speak, you will have 20 seconds to record. You should respond as fully and as appropriately as possible.

1. Conversation

You are chatting with your friend, a senior high school student in China, about preparing gifts.

Directions: You will be asked to speak in Chinese on different topics in the following two questions. In each case, imagine you are making an oral presentation to your family in Chinese. First, you will read and hear the topic for your presentation. You will have 4 minutes to prepare your presentation. Then you will have 2 minutes to record your presentation. Your presentation should be as complete as possible.

2. Cultural Presentation

In your presentation, describe how Chinese people celebrate the Dragon Boat Festival. You should mention details such as the special food (*Zongzi*), and the activities (the dragon boat race itself).

3. Event Plan

You have the opportunity to plan a three-day holiday for your family. In your presentation, explain to your parents what you suggest doing. You may compare your ideas with other options and explain why you think your ideas are better.

UNIT FIVE
LESSON 9
Travel and Transportation
Planning a Trip to China

Section One

I.   Multiple Choice (Listen to the dialogs)

Note: In this part, you may NOT move back and forth among questions.

Directions: In this part, you will hear several short conversations or parts of conversations followed by four choices, designated (A), (B), (C), and (D). Choose the one that continues or completes the conversation in a logical and culturally appropriate manner. You will have 5 seconds to answer each question.

1.	(A)	(B)	(C)	(D)	5.	(A)	(B)	(C)	(D)
2.	(A)	(B)	(C)	(D)	6.	(A)	(B)	(C)	(D)
3.	(A)	(B)	(C)	(D)	7.	(A)	(B)	(C)	(D)
4.	(A)	(B)	(C)	(D)	8.	(A)	(B)	(C)	(D)

II.   Multiple Choice (Listen to the selections)

Note: In this part, you may move back and forth only among the questions associated with the current listening selection.

Directions: In this part, you will listen to several selections in Chinese. For each selection, you will be told whether it will be played once or twice. You may take notes as you listen. After listening to each selection, you will see questions in English. For each question, choose the response that is best according to the selection. You will have 12 seconds to answer each question.

Selection 1

1.   Why is the flight delayed?
   (A) Because the weather is very bad.
   (B) Because there has been a security alert.
   (C) Because the plane needs immediate maintenance.
   (D) Because some passengers haven't boarded the plane yet.

2. When will the plane take off?

(A) In about 30 minutes.

(B) In about an hour.

(C) In about three hours.

(D) It has yet to be confirmed.

3. According to the message, which of the following statements is TRUE?

(A) The destination of the flight is San Francisco.

(B) The plane needs to be replaced for this flight.

(C) Passengers are advised to stay in the departure lounge until further notice.

(D) The flight will transit in New York.

Selection 2

4. This conversation would probably take place _____ .

(A) at a customer service counter

(B) at the main gate of a school

(C) on a bus

(D) at a bus stop

5. How many times should the man change buses?

(A) Once.

(B) Twice.

(C) Three times.

(D) It's not necessary to change bus.

6. Where should the man take the bus?

(A) At the bus stop next to the school

(B) At the bus station

(C) Across the street

(D) Right in front of the shop

Selection 3

7. Why is Xiao He calling Mr. Li?

(A) She wants to confirm accommodation details with him.

(B) She wants to invite him to join her on her trip to Guilin.

(C) She wants to inform him about his flight schedule to Guilin.

(D) She wants to tell him her contact number in Guilin.

8. According to the message, which of the following statements is TRUE?
    (A) Mr. Li will get a free shuttle transfer from the airport to the hotel.
    (B) Xiao He will wait for Mr. Li at the hotel lobby.
    (C) Mr. Li is going for a three-day trip to Guilin.
    (D) Xiao He has already booked a room for Mr. Li.

9. When will Mr. Li meet the travel agent?
    (A) At 8 am on 26th
    (B) At 8 pm on 26th
    (C) At 8 am on 27th
    (D) At 8 pm on 27th

Selection 4

10. What happened to the woman?
    (A) She lost her cell phone.
    (B) She lost her purse.
    (C) She left her bag in the subway.
    (D) She lost her identity card.

11. What does the man suggest the woman do?
    (A) Make a police report.
    (B) Call her parents.
    (C) Call the subway's customer service hotline.
    (D) Go back to the subway station.

12. According to the conversation, which of the following is TRUE?
    (A) The man is a passer-by.
    (B) The woman has no idea where her belongings might be.
    (C) The woman is so panicky she doesn't know what to do.
    (D) The man guessed that the woman dropped her belongings on the street.

III. Multiple Choice (Reading)

Note: In this part, you may move back and forth among all the questions.

Directions: You will read several selections in Chinese. Each selection is accompanied by a number of questions in English. For each question, choose the response that is best according to the selection.

Read this notice.

[Simplified-character version]	[Traditional-character version]
登山活动通知	登山活動通知
为了丰富大家的课余生活，本协会将于本月二十五日（本周六）组织大家去香山观赏红叶。想参加此次活动的同学，请到学生会办公室报名。 　　如果您还希望通过此次活动加入登山协会，请在报名时带上一张一寸的照片。 　　本次活动收取门票费五元，交通费由学生会负责。报名截止时间为本周五中午十二点整。参加者请于周六上午八点准时在校东门门口集合，八点十分我们准时出发。建议大家穿运动服和运动鞋，以便登山。 <div align="right">校登山协会 十月二十日</div>	爲了豐富大家的課餘生活，本協會將於本月二十五日（本週六）組織大家去香山觀賞紅葉。想參加此次活動的同學，請到學生會辦公室報名。 　　如果您還希望通過此次活動加入登山協會，請在報名時帶上一張一寸的照片。 　　本次活動收取門票費五元，交通費由學生會負責。報名截止時間爲本週五中午十二點整。參加者請於週六上午八點準時在校東門門口集合，八點十分我們準時出發。建議大家穿運動服和運動鞋，以便登山。 <div align="right">校登山協會 十月二十日</div>

1. Which of the following is mentioned in the notice?
    (A) Each participant needs to pay a 5-*yuan* admission charge.
    (B) The registration venue is the mountain climbing club's office.
    (C) Members of the mountain climbing club have priority for registration.
    (D) Registration is open until October 24 12:30 pm.

2. What should students do if they want to join the mountain climbing club?
    (A) They need to register before October 23.
    (B) They need to pay 5 *yuan* for the membership fee.
    (C) They need to fill in a form which can be downloaded online.
    (D) They need to bring along a photo when registering for activities.

3. According to the notice, which of the following is TRUE?

(A) The participants should meet at 8:00 am at the school's west gate.

(B) The participant should put on hats to prevent sunburn.

(C) The participants should wear sports clothes and sneakers.

(D) The participants need to arrive 15 minutes before the official set off time.

Read this poster.

[Simplified-character version]	[Traditional-character version]
参观须知	參觀須知
开馆时间： 上午9:00 —下午6:00 （周六、周日照常开放，周一休馆）	開館時間： 上午9:00 — 下午6:00 （週六、週日照常開放，週一休館）
门票： 成人50元；学生与60岁以上（含60岁）的老人凭证件半价；1.2米以下儿童免费。10人以上团体票每人35元。门票当天一次有效。	門票： 成人50元；學生與60歲以上（含60歲）的老人憑證件半價；1.2米以下兒童免費。10人以上團體票每人35元。門票當天一次有效。
请将随身携带的包裹存放到寄存处（钱包、相机、手机等贵重物品除外）。	請將隨身攜帶的包裹存放到寄存處（錢包、相機、手機等貴重物品除外）。
严禁携带易燃、易爆物品入内。 爱护馆内文物，严禁乱涂乱画。 馆内禁止吸烟，请勿随地吐痰。 请照顾好自己的小孩，以免走失。	嚴禁攜帶易燃、易爆物品入內。 愛護館內文物，嚴禁亂塗亂畫。 館內禁止吸煙，請勿隨地吐痰。 請照顧好自己的小孩，以免走失。

4. What time does the museum open on Saturdays?

(A) At 8:30 am

(B) At 9:00 am

(C) At 10:00 am

(D) At 12:00 pm

5. How much would a college student have to pay if they forget to bring their student card along?

(A) 25 *yuan*

(B) 35 *yuan*

(C) 40 *yuan*

(D) 50 *yuan*

6. According to the notice, which of the following statements is TRUE?

(A) People cannot bring their handbags in with them.

(B) Children shorter than 1.2 meters need to pay 25 *yuan* for a ticket.

(C) The museum closes on Tuesdays.

(D) Photography is not allowed in the museum.

Read this passage.

[Simplified-character version]	[Traditional-character version]
我和妻子从印度来北京已经快一年了。上星期六的晚上，房东许先生一家约我们一起去吃火锅，我和妻子挺高兴，觉得机会终于来了。以前好几次和房东夫妇下馆子，都是他们付的帐，因为在中国人吃饭时常见的"结帐比赛"中，我们缺乏取胜的技巧。我们在餐馆吃饭时，经常会看到这样的景象：两三个人同时去抢帐单，最后总是只有一个人胜利。以前在这种比赛中，许先生总是赢家，这次我们下决心要反败为胜。我们计划等吃得差不多时，我妻子借口上洗手间，偷偷去结帐。吃了大概半小时后，我妻子按照计划起身到洗手间，然后转到收银台结帐，可是女服务员说："跟你们一起来的那位老先生半个小时前已经把帐结过了。"	我和妻子從印度來北京已經快一年了。上星期六的晚上，房東許先生一家約我們一起去吃火鍋，我和妻子挺高興，覺得機會終於來了。以前好幾次和房東夫婦下館子，都是他們付的帳，因爲在中國人吃飯時常見的"結帳比賽"中，我們缺乏取勝的技巧。我們在餐館吃飯時，經常會看到這樣的景象：兩三個人同時去搶帳單，最後總是只有一個人勝利。以前在這種比賽中，許先生總是贏家，這次我們下決心要反敗爲勝。我們計劃等吃得差不多時，我妻子借口上洗手間，偷偷去結帳。吃了大概半小時後，我妻子按照計劃起身到洗手間，然後轉到收銀臺結帳，可是女服務員說："跟你們一起來的那位老先生半個小時前已經把帳結過了。"

7. Why is the author of this passage happy to have a hotpot with Mr. and Mrs. Xu?

(A) Because Mr. and Mrs. Xu have agreed to teach him and his wife how to eat hotpot.

(B) Because he and his wife finally have the chance to give Mr. and Mrs. Xu a treat.

(C) Because Mr. Xu always tell stories about Chinese culture during meals.

(D) Because he and his wife like eating hotpot very much.

8. What is "结帐比赛（結帳比賽）"?

(A) It is a popular form of entertainment in China.

(B) It is a math contest.

(C) It is an activity Chinese people like to do while eating hotpot.

(D) It is a description of how Chinese people compete with one another to pay the bill for meals.

9. During dinner, the author's wife excused herself to go to the rest room because _____ .

   (A) she had a stomach ache

   (B) she wanted to touch up her make-up

   (C) she wanted to pay the bill in advance

   (D) she wanted to make a phone call

10. Who was the winner of the "contest"?

   (A) Mr. Xu

   (B) Mrs. Xu

   (C) The author of this passage

   (D) The author's wife

Read this letter.

[Simplified-character version]

哥哥:

　　最近好吗?

　　我上个星期去了一趟内蒙古, 你听说过这个地方吗? 它在北京的北边, 坐火车很快就到了。那儿和北京的风景完全不一样, 全是大草原。蒙古族人的房子特别有意思, 就像是一个个鼓起的白色气球, 又大又圆, 当地人把这样的房子叫 "蒙古包"。不过现在很多人已经不住 "蒙古包" 了。我这次去的时候, 正赶上草原上的一个赛马节。他们告诉我, 这儿的男人如果不会骑马, 就算不上真正的男子汉。所以, 虽然我以前从没骑过马, 这次还是试了一下, 结果差点儿从马背上摔下来, 不过真有意思。我还喝了当地特产的 "奶茶"。这种茶居然是咸的, 你以前肯定没听说过。除此之外还有其他很多有趣的事情, 等我下次再和你说。

　　　祝
生活愉快!

　　　　　　　　　　弟: 小强
　　　　　　　　　2006年7月6日

[Traditional-character version]

哥哥:

　　最近好嗎?

　　我上個星期去了一趟內蒙古, 你聽說過這個地方嗎? 它在北京的北邊, 坐火車很快就到了。那兒和北京的風景完全不一樣, 全是大草原。蒙古族人的房子特別有意思, 就像是一個個鼓起的白色汽球, 又大又圓, 當地人把這樣的房子叫 "蒙古包"。不過現在很多人已經不住 "蒙古包" 了。我這次去的時候, 正趕上草原上的一個賽馬節。他們告訴我, 這兒的男人如果不會騎馬, 就算不上真正的男子漢。所以, 雖然我以前從沒騎過馬, 這次還是試了一下, 結果差點兒從馬背上摔下來, 不過真有意思。我還喝了當地特產的 "奶茶"。這種茶居然是鹹的, 你以前肯定沒聽說過。除此之外還有其他很多有趣的事情, 等我下次再和你說。

　　　祝
生活愉快!

　　　　　　　　　　弟: 小强
　　　　　　　　　2006年7月6日

11. According to the passage, what is so special about Mongolian houses?

    (A) The inside of the houses are cold during the day and warm at night.

    (B) They are painted white so that they stand out.

    (C) They look like giant balloons.

    (D) They are built on grassland.

12. Why did Xiao Qiang learn to ride a horse?

    (A) Because he likes horses very much.

    (B) Because it's the local custom that every man should be able to ride a horse.

    (C) Because he needed to ride a horse for his job.

    (D) Because he wanted to participate in a horseback riding contest.

13. What does Xiao Qiang say about the milk tea?

    (A) He is surprised that it tastes salty.

    (B) He thinks it tastes the same as other milk teas.

    (C) He doesn't really like it.

    (D) He thinks it is very sweet.

Read this passage.

[Simplified-character version]	[Traditional-character version]
大家好！感谢大家的信任，选择我们新星旅行社。我是导游宋祥，今天由我代替小王继续带领大家游览故宫和天坛。首先我说一下我们的时间安排：上午8:30先到故宫，我们从南门进去，游览时间为三个小时。11点半我们在南门集合，然后一起去品尝附近的风味小吃。1:00我们坐车去天坛，1:30到达。天坛比较大，所以参观的时候大家一定要抓紧时间。下午5:00我们在天坛的东门集合。为了减轻大家的负担，大家游览的时候可以把行李放在座位上，但我们建议您随身携带贵重的物品。感谢大家对我们的支持！	大家好！感謝大家的信任，選擇我們新星旅行社。我是導遊宋祥，今天由我代替小王繼續帶領大家遊覽故宮和天壇。首先我說一下我們的時間安排：上午8:30先到故宮，我們從南門進去，遊覽時間爲三個小時。11點半我們在南門集合，然後一起去品嚐附近的風味小吃。1:00我們坐車去天壇，1:30到達。天壇比較大，所以參觀的時候大家一定要抓緊時間。下午5:00我們在天壇的東門集合。爲了減輕大家的負擔，大家遊覽的時候可以把行李放在座位上，但我們建議您隨身攜帶貴重的物品。感謝大家對我們的支持！

14. Where are the tourists likely to be at 1:20 pm?

   (A) In a restaurant

   (B) On the bus

   (C) At the Forbidden City

   (D) At the Temple of Heaven

15. From the passage, we can infer that _____ .

   (A) the Temple of Heaven is much bigger than the Forbidden City.

   (B) the tourists will be having a huge lunch at a famous restaurant.

   (C) the tourists are on their first day of the trip.

   (D) it takes about 15 minutes to go to the Temple of Heaven from the Forbidden City.

16. The guide says that the time allocated to the Temple of Heaven _____ .

   (A) is more than enough

   (B) is a bit tight

   (C) can be adjusted if the tourists want

   (D) is just right

17. According to the passage, which of the following statements is TRUE?

   (A) The tourists will be having lunch at 12:30 pm.

   (B) The tourists should gather at the south gate after they visit the Forbidden City.

   (C) The tourists can spend four hours at the Forbidden City.

   (D) The tourists are advised to leave their personal belongings in the bus.

Read this public sign.

[Simplified-character version]   [Traditional-character version]

雪天路滑，注意安全   雪天路滑，注意安全

18. Where would this sign most likely appear?

   (A) In a parking lot

   (B) On the side of a bus

   (C) At the side of a freeway

   (D) At a train station

19. What is the purpose of this sign?

(A) To remind people to wear their seatbelts.

(B) To remind people to be careful.

(C) To remind people not to forget their belongings.

(D) To remind people not to drive after drinking alcohol.

Read this public sign.

[Simplified-character version]   [Traditional-character version]

请您保管好随身携带的物品   請您保管好隨身攜帶的物品

20. Where would this sign most likely appear?

(A) In an office

(B) In a carpark

(C) In a dormitory

(D) In a train station

Read this public sign.

[Simplified-character version]   [Traditional-character version]

干旱季节, 禁止野炊   乾旱季節, 禁止野炊

21. Where would this sign most likely appear?

(A) At the roadside

(B) By a river

(C) On a beach

(D) In a forest

22. The sign is to remind people _____ .

(A) to act responsibly

(B) to guard against fire

(C) to stay away from the river

(D) to be wary of poisonous insects

Section Two

I. Free Response (Writing)

Note: In this part, you may NOT move back and forth among questions.

Directions: You will be asked to write in Chinese in a variety of ways. In each case, you will be asked to write for a specific purpose and to a specific person. You should write in as complete and as culturally appropriate a manner as possible, taking into account the purpose and the person described.

1. Story Narration

The four pictures present a story. Imagine you are writing the story to a friend. Narrate a complete story as suggested by the pictures. Give your story a beginning, a middle, and an end.

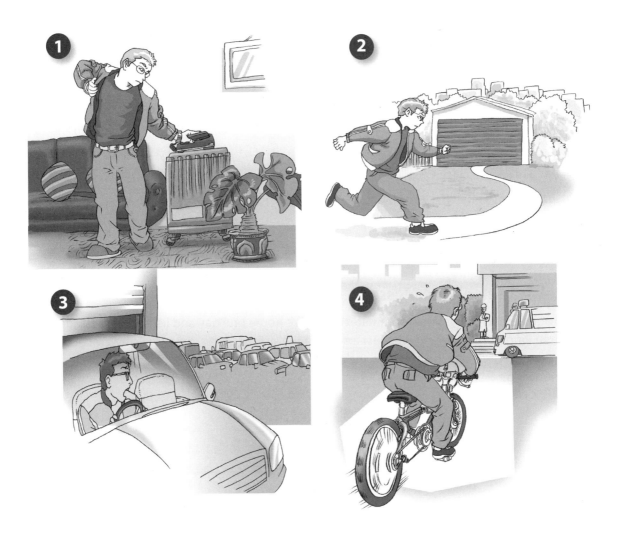

2. Personal Letter

Imagine you received a letter from a pen pal. He thinks the idea of driving to school — which you mentioned in your last letter — is very interesting and would like to know more about it. Write a reply in letter format. Tell your pen pal about modes of transport high school students in the United States use to go to school and their reasons for doing so. Also mention how you go to school and your reasons.

3. E-Mail Response

Read this e-mail from a friend and then type a response.

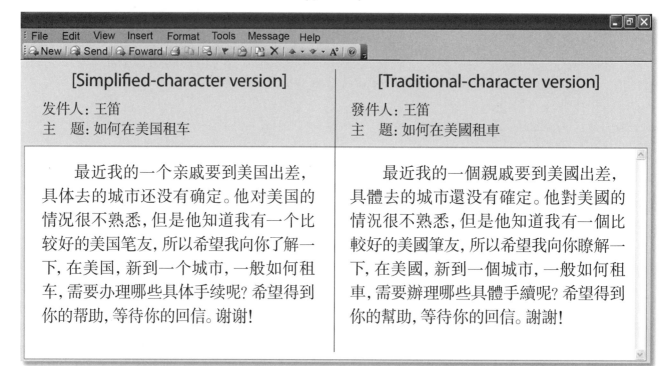

File   Edit   View   Insert   Format   Tools   Message   Help

New   Send   Foward

[Simplified-character version]

发件人：王笛
主　题：如何在美国租车

　　最近我的一个亲戚要到美国出差，具体去的城市还没有确定。他对美国的情况很不熟悉，但是他知道我有一个比较好的美国笔友，所以希望我向你了解一下，在美国，新到一个城市，一般如何租车，需要办理哪些具体手续呢? 希望得到你的帮助，等待你的回信。谢谢!

[Traditional-character version]

發件人：王笛
主　題：如何在美國租車

　　最近我的一個親戚要到美國出差，具體去的城市還沒有確定。他對美國的情況很不熟悉，但是他知道我有一個比較好的美國筆友，所以希望我向你瞭解一下，在美國，新到一個城市，一般如何租車，需要辦理哪些具體手續呢? 希望得到你的幫助，等待你的回信。謝謝!

4. Relay a Telephone Message

Imagine Zhou Ping is your roommate. You arrive home one day and listen to a message for Zhou Ping from her friend who just arrived in the United States. You will listen twice to the message. Then relay the message, including the important details, by typing a note to Zhou Ping.

II. Free Response (Speaking)

Note: In this part, you may NOT move back and forth among questions.

Directions: You will participate in a simulated conversation. Each time it is your turn to speak, you will have 20 seconds to record. You should respond as fully and as appropriately as possible.

1. Conversation

You will have a conversation with a visa officer at the Chinese embassy about your holiday trip to China.

Directions: You will be asked to speak in Chinese on different topics in the following two questions. In each case, imagine you are making an oral presentation to your class in Chinese. First, you will read and hear the topic for your presentation. You will have 4 minutes to prepare your presentation. Then you will have 2 minutes to record your presentation. Your presentation should be as complete as possible.

2. Cultural Presentation

The Silk Road was an ancient route that came into existence over 2000 years ago. Through this road, China developed economic and cultural ties to the West. There is a famous scenic spot along this route called Dunhuang. In your presentation, explain what you know about Dunhuang.

3. Event Plan

You have the opportunity to plan a five-day holiday to China. In your presentation, explain your plan including the budget, the destinations (cities and scenic spots), the modes of transport and the hotels you choose, the reasons for your choices, and the pros and cons of different choices.

UNIT FIVE LESSON 10 Travel and Transportation
I Climbed the Great Wall

Section One

I. Multiple Choice (Listen to the dialogs)

Note: In this part, you may NOT move back and forth among questions.

Directions: In this part, you will hear several short conversations or parts of conversations followed by four choices, designated (A), (B), (C), and (D). Choose the one that continues or completes the conversation in a logical and culturally appropriate manner. You will have 5 seconds to answer each question.

1.	(A)	(B)	(C)	(D)	5.	(A)	(B)	(C)	(D)
2.	(A)	(B)	(C)	(D)	6.	(A)	(B)	(C)	(D)
3.	(A)	(B)	(C)	(D)	7.	(A)	(B)	(C)	(D)
4.	(A)	(B)	(C)	(D)	8.	(A)	(B)	(C)	(D)

II. Multiple Choice (Listen to the selections)

Note: In this part, you may move back and forth only among the questions associated with the current listening selection.

Directions: In this part, you will listen to several selections in Chinese. For each selection, you will be told whether it will be played once or twice. You may take notes as you listen. After listening to each selection, you will see questions in English. For each question, choose the response that is best according to the selection. You will have 12 seconds to answer each question.

Selection 1
1. Where are the people going?
   (A) To the theater
   (B) To the train station
   (C) To the sports stadium
   (D) To the airport

2. Why does the woman say they should NOT set off for their destination now?

(A) Because it is Saturday and there should not be too much traffic.

(B) Because the place is not very far away.

(C) Because she isn't ready yet.

(D) Because they haven't had dinner yet.

3. What is the man's opinion?

(A) He prefers to set off earlier just in case of traffic.

(B) He thinks they can eat dinner on the way.

(C) He is fine with leaving slightly late.

(D) He worries it will be hard to find a parking space if they arrive too late.

Selection 2

4. According to the message, which of the following is TRUE?

(A) The train operates 18 hours a day.

(B) This announcement takes place at a railway station.

(C) The earliest train is at 5:00 am.

(D) The next stop is Fuxingmen.

5. When is the last train?

(A) At 11:00 pm

(B) At 11:15 pm

(C) At 11:30 pm

(D) At 1:45 am

6. If you are on Line 1 now and want to transfer to Line 2, where should you get off?

(A) At Xizhimen

(B) At Tiananmen

(C) At Fuxingmen

(D) At Fuchengmen

Selection 3

7. Why does the man approach the woman?

(A) He needs help with the ticket vending machine.

(B) He wants to change some coins.

(C) He wants someone to take a photograph for him.

(D) He wants to ask for directions.

8. From the conversation, we know that the man _____ .

    (A) loves to travel by himself.

    (B) is an exchange student from the United States.

    (C) is traveling in China with his family.

    (D) is traveling in China with his friends.

9. Why does the man speak Chinese so well?

    (A) He has lived in China before.

    (B) He has very good Chinese teachers.

    (C) He travels to China frequently.

    (D) His parents are Chinese.

Selection 4

10. What did Lingling leave in the taxi?

    (A) Her purse

    (B) Her keys

    (C) Her camera

    (D) Her cell phone

11. How did Lingling find the telephone number of the taxi company?

    (A) Her friend helped her check for it.

    (B) She found it on the Internet.

    (C) It was printed on her receipt.

    (D) She found it in the telephone directory.

12. According to the message, which of the following is TRUE?

    (A) Lingling called her brother to tell him what happened to her.

    (B) Lingling took a taxi to meet her friends at the museum.

    (C) Lingling's friends thought it would be impossible to get her belongings back.

    (D) Lingling realized that she had left her belongings in the taxi in the afternoon.

Selection 5

13. What are the two people looking at?

    (A) A photo taken by the man's brother.

    (B) A postcard from the man's brother.

    (C) A website forwarded by the man's brother.

    (D) A video sent by the man's brother.

14. The man's brother is probably studying in _____ .

    (A) Shanghai

    (B) Xi'an

    (C) Beijing

    (D) Hangzhou

15. According to the conversation, which of the following is TRUE?

    (A) The man's parents will visit him next month.

    (B) The man will visit his brother with his parents next month.

    (C) The man's brother has been living in China for over two months.

    (D) The man's brother visited the Forbidden City during the summer vacation.

III. Multiple Choice (Reading)

Note: In this part, you may move back and forth among all the questions.

Directions: You will read several selections in Chinese. Each selection is accompanied by a number of questions in English. For each question, choose the response that is best according to the selection.

Read this note.

[Simplified-character version]	[Traditional-character version]
姐姐： 　　刚才李丽来过一趟，她说今年春节期间的火车票可以提前五天买。我算了一下时间，今天可以买我们出发那天的票，所以我现在就去火车站，我担心去晚了买不到票。如果超过七点我还没回来，那你就不用等我吃晚饭了，我到时候再给你打电话。如果我回来得早，我们就一起去附近新开的那家川菜馆吃晚饭。 　　　　　　　　　　　　文文 　　　　　　　　　　　1月20日16时	姐姐： 　　剛才李麗來過一趟，她說今年春節期間的火車票可以提前五天買。我算了一下時間，今天可以買我們出發那天的票，所以我現在就去火車站，我擔心去晚了買不到票。如果超過七點我還沒回來，那你就不用等我吃晚飯了，我到時候再給你打電話。如果我回來得早，我們就一起去附近新開的那家川菜館吃晚飯。 　　　　　　　　　　　　文文 　　　　　　　　　　　1月20日16時

1. Why does Wenwen write a note to her sister?
   (A) To tell her that she will be home after 7:00 pm.
   (B) To tell her that she will make a reservation at the restaurant.
   (C) To tell her that she will buy the train tickets.
   (D) To tell her that she will go out with Lili.

2. When will the sisters be leaving?
   (A) Tomorrow
   (B) In 3 days
   (C) In 5 days
   (D) In a week

3. Which of the following can be inferred from the note?
   (A) People normally can buy train tickets during Chinese New Year a week in advance.
   (B) Wenwen just had a phone conversation with Lili.
   (C) There is a new Sichuan restaurant near the sisters' house.
   (D) Wenwen's sister will be having her dinner at 7:00 pm.

Read this advertisement.

[Simplified-character version]	[Traditional-character version]
转眼又到年底了,元旦您有什么打算? 在家看电视? 上网? 工作? 您还在过这样没有新意的新年吗? 请参加我们的海南之旅吧。您可以享受阳光灿烂的海滩、风味独特的海南美食,还有热情周到的酒店服务。别再犹豫了,现在就给我们打电话! 带上您的朋友,一起去海南过新年吧! 两人以上报名可以享受9折优惠! 旅行时间: 12月30日—1月3日 价格: 3999元/人 电话: 010—82196785 联系人: 中国国际旅行社　张先生	轉眼又到年底了,元旦您有什麼打算? 在家看電視? 上網? 工作? 您還在過這樣沒有新意的新年嗎? 請參加我們的海南之旅吧。您可以享受陽光燦爛的海灘、風味獨特的海南美食,還有熱情周到的酒店服務。別再猶豫了,現在就給我們打電話! 帶上您的朋友,一起去海南過新年吧! 兩人以上報名可以享受9折優惠! 旅行時間: 12月30日—1月3日 價格: 3999元/人 電話: 010—82196785 聯繫人: 中國國際旅行社　張先生

4. According to the advertisement, which of the following do peoeple NOT usually do during the New Year holiday?

   (A) Surf the Internet at home.

   (B) Travel.

   (C) Work.

   (D) Watch TV.

5. Under what circumstance will the travel agency give a discount?

   (A) If more than two people travel together.

   (B) If the tour is booked by December 3.

   (C) If the cost of the tour is paid in cash.

   (D) If you are one of the first six people to sign up for the tour.

Read this passage.

[Simplified-character version]	[Traditional-character version]
北京的道路很有意思，如果从高空往下看，你会发现道路把城市划分为一个个方块儿，非常整齐，人们很容易从东南西北四个方向对它进行区分。所以在北京问路的时候，北京人一般不说"往左拐""往右拐"之类的话，而是会告诉你"往东走"或是"往北走"等等。此外，围绕着城市中心，北京还修建了很多环状公路，叫做"环线"。目前，北京已经有六条环线了。这些道路让北京的交通变得四通八达，非常便利！	北京的道路很有意思，如果從高空往下看，你會發現道路把城市劃分爲一個個方塊兒，非常整齊，人們很容易從東南西北四個方向對它進行區分。所以在北京問路的時候，北京人一般不説"往左拐""往右拐"之類的話，而是會告訴你"往東走"或是"往北走"等等。此外，圍繞著城市中心，北京還修建了很多環狀公路，叫做"環線"。目前，北京已經有六條環線了。這些道路讓北京的交通變得四通八達，非常便利！

6. Why do people who live in Beijing always give road directions by using "north", "south", "east" or "west"?

   (A) Because Chinese people are usually very familiar with compass reading.

   (B) Because roads in Beijing are divided into a grid.

   (C) Because roads in Beijing are very complicated.

   (D) Because there are many *hutongs* in Beijing and many of them don't have names.

7. According to the passage, which of the following is TRUE?

   (A) The "rings" are ring-shaped roads that surround the city center.

   (B) The "rings" are built in order to direct traffic flow during peak hours.

   (C) The "rings" are not very convenient and make journeys longer.

   (D) There are more than six "rings" in Beijing now.

8. The author thinks that the transportation system in Beijing _____.

    (A) should have been planned better

    (B) is very convenient

    (C) is very complicated

    (D) is not as good as it used to be

Read this passage.

[Simplified-character version]	[Traditional-character version]
丽江是中国云南省西北部的一个美丽的城市。这里居住着纳西族、白族、藏族等很多少数民族，其中以纳西族为主。丽江不仅风景优美，还具有许多与众不同的特色。比如，从古至今，丽江都是一座没有围墙的城市。一个城市没有围墙，这在中国的城市当中是非常少有的。这是为什么呢？原来很久以前，丽江的统治者姓"木"，他认为，如果给丽江修建了城墙，就好像是在"木"字外边加了一个"口"字，就变成"困"字了，不吉利，所以丽江一直没有城墙。	麗江是中國雲南省西北部的一個美麗的城市。這裏居住著納西族、白族、藏族等很多少數民族，其中以納西族爲主。麗江不僅風景優美，還具有許多與衆不同的特色。比如，從古至今，麗江都是一座沒有圍牆的城市。一個城市沒有圍牆，這在中國的城市當中是非常少有的。這是爲什麼呢？原來很久以前，麗江的統治者姓"木"，他認爲，如果給麗江修建了城牆，就好像是在"木"字外邊加了一個"口"字，就變成"困"字了，不吉利，所以麗江一直沒有城牆。

9. Lijiang has the greatest population of which minority group?

    (A) The Naxi people

    (B) The Bai people

    (C) The Zhang people

    (D) The Dai people

10. According to the passage, which of the following is TRUE?

    (A) Lijiang is situated in the southwest of Yunnan Province.

    (B) Minorities only make up a small fraction of the total population of Lijiang.

    (C) Lijiang is the only city in China without city walls.

    (D) Lijiang has breathtaking scenery.

11. Why didn't the ancient ruler of Lijiang build city walls?

    (A) Because he was afraid that city walls would bring bad luck.

    (B) Because he lived in a peaceful time and it was unnecessary.

    (C) Because he thought building city walls would waste a lot of money.

    (D) Because he wanted Lijiang to be different from other cities.

Read this advertisement.

[Simplified-character version]

招聘广告

由于工作需要，本社现招聘导游3人，主要负责北京市内各景点的导游接待工作。要求：1.男女不限，身体健康，年龄在22~30岁之间；2.普通话标准，英语口语流利，有较强的语言表达能力；3.工作认真负责，有一年以上导游工作经验者优先；4.熟悉北京地区各旅游景点的情况。工资面议。

本次招聘活动从即日起到本月15日结束，有意者请尽快将简历寄到北京西三环华宝大厦1016室，邮政编码100859；或发送至beijingtravel@hotmail.com。我们会及时和您联系，面试时间将另行通知。

北京旅行社人力资源部
2006年11月1日

[Traditional-character version]

招聘廣告

由於工作需要，本社現招聘導遊3人，主要負責北京市內各景點的導遊接待工作。要求：1.男女不限，身體健康，年齡在22~30歲之間；2.普通話標準，英語口語流利，有較強的語言表達能力；3.工作認真負責，有一年以上導遊工作經驗者優先；4.熟悉北京地區各旅遊景點的情況。工資面議。

本次招聘活動從即日起到本月15日結束，有意者請儘快將簡歷寄到北京西三環華寶大廈1016室，郵政編碼100859；或發送至beijingtravel@hotmail.com。我們會及時和您聯繫，面試時間將另行通知。

北京旅行社人力資源部
2006年11月1日

12. Which kind of applicants will have priority for shortlisting?

   (A) Applicants who are aged between 22–30.

   (B) Applicants who can speak three foreign languages.

   (C) Applicants who have working experiences as tour guides.

   (D) Applicants who are familiar with tourist spots in Beijing.

13. When must applications reach the company?

   (A) By November 7

   (B) By November 12

   (C) By November 15

   (D) By November 21

14. What does "工资面议（工資面議）" mean?

   (A) Salaries will be agreed between employers and employees.

   (B) Applicants must write their expected salaries in their resume.

   (C) Salaries will be commensurate with skills and experience.

   (D) Salaries are fixed by the employer.

15. How many ways are available for applicants to send in their resumes?

(A) One

(B) Two

(C) Three

(D) Four

Read this passage.

[Simplified-character version]	[Traditional-character version]
外出旅游, 你会选择什么样的旅游方式呢? 去旅行社报名跟团旅游? 还是自己安排一切的 "自助游"? 如果你只会这两种方式, 说明你已经落伍了。最近, 一种新的旅游方式在网络上流行起来, 叫 "互换旅游"。什么是 "互换旅游" 呢? 举例来说, 陈先生住在北京, 但他最近想去成都旅游, 李先生住在成都, 他最近却想去北京旅游, 于是他们就可以在约定的时间内互相交换住房, 到对方的城市去旅游。这样的方式不仅花费很少, 而且还可以让人在其他的城市找到 "家" 的感觉。	外出旅遊, 你會選擇什麼樣的旅遊方式呢? 去旅行社報名跟團旅遊? 還是自己安排一切的 "自助遊"? 如果你只會這兩種方式, 说明你已經落伍了。最近, 一種新的旅遊方式在網絡上流行起來, 叫 "互換旅遊"。什麼是 "互換旅遊" 呢? 舉例來說, 陳先生住在北京, 但他最近想去成都旅遊, 李先生住在成都, 他最近卻想去北京旅遊, 於是他們就可以在約定的時間內互相交換住房, 到對方的城市去旅遊。這樣的方式不僅花費很少, 而且還可以讓人在其他的城市找到 "家" 的感覺。

16. What the purpose of this passage?

(A) To outline advantages and disadvantages of different modes of travel.

(B) To describe a new travel option.

(C) To encourage people to travel during the holidays.

(D) To recommending Beijing and Chengdu as travel destinations.

17. How many types of travel options are mentioned in the passage?

(A) Two

(B) Three

(C) Four

(D) Five

Read this diary.

[Simplified-character version]	[Traditional-character version]
2006年12月3日　晴	2006年12月3日　晴
今天是星期天, 我和王乐一块儿去了故宫。故宫确实很大, 很壮观, 虽然我已经多次在电视上看过, 但今天第一次实地参观, 我还是觉得很激动。我拍了很多照片, 但也有些遗憾: 由于故宫正进行大规模修整, 我不能进 "太和殿" 参观。这个宫殿不仅是故宫里最大的建筑, 也是以前皇帝举行重大活动的地方。王乐告诉我, 从2002年10月起, 故宫就开始进行整修了, 这次大规模整修可能要持续到2020年才能全部结束。我想今后的故宫会比我今天看到的更漂亮!	今天是星期天, 我和王樂一塊兒去了故宮。故宮確實很大, 很壯觀, 雖然我已經多次在電視上看過, 但今天第一次實地參觀, 我還是覺得很激動。我拍了很多照片, 但也有些遺憾: 由於故宮正進行大規模修整, 我不能進 "太和殿" 參觀。這個宮殿不僅是故宮裏最大的建築, 也是以前皇帝舉行重大活動的地方。王樂告訴我, 從2002年10月起, 故宮就開始進行整修了, 這次大規模整修可能要持續到2020年才能全部結束。我想今後的故宮會比我今天看到的更漂亮!

18. According to the diary, which of the following is TRUE?

    (A) The author is excited because this is his first visit to the Forbidden City.

    (B) The Hall of Supreme Harmony is the place where emperors held regular meetings.

    (C) The author visited the Forbidden City on Saturday with a friend.

    (D) The Hall of Supreme Harmony is the second largest building in the museum.

19. Why did the author feel upset when visiting the Forbidden City?

    (A) Because there were too many visitors and everywhere was crowded.

    (B) Because most of the places in the Forbidden City were under repair.

    (C) Because he couldn't visit the Hall of Supreme Harmony.

    (D) Because the Forbidden City closed early so he couldn't see everything.

20. How long will the restoration work to the Palace Museum take?

    (A) 8 years

    (B) One or two years

    (C) Almost 10 years

    (D) More than 15 years

Read this public sign.

[Simplified-character version]   [Traditional-character version]

谢绝拍照   謝絕拍照

21. Where would this sign most likely appear?

(A) In a temple

(B) In a park

(C) At a cemetery

(D) At a sports stadium

22. What is the purpose of this sign?

(A) To remind people to hold on to their camera.

(B) To tell people that taking photos is forbidden.

(C) To prevent people from bringing in cameras.

(D) To tell people not to use a flash when taking photos.

Read this public sign.

Simplified-character version   Traditional-character version

来客请登记   來客請登記

23. Where would this sign most likely appear?

(A) In a restaurant

(B) At a sports field

(C) In an office building

(D) At the airport

24. What does this sign mean?

(A) Guests should check in first at the reception.

(B) Participants must register before the games start.

(C) Passengers are advised to get ready for boarding at the specified time.

(D) Visitors must register at the specified area.

Section Two

I. Free Response (Writing)

Note: In this part, you may NOT move back and forth among questions.

Directions: You will be asked to write in Chinese in a variety of ways. In each case, you will be asked to write for a specific purpose and to a specific person. You should write in as complete and as culturally appropriate a manner as possible, taking into account the purpose and the person described.

1. Story Narration

The four pictures present a story. Imagine you are writing the story to a friend. Write a complete story as suggested by the pictures. Give your story a beginning, a middle, and an end.

2. Personal Letter

Imagine you received a letter from a pen pal. In the letter, he expresses interest in learning about the differences between the east and west coasts of the United States. Write a reply in letter format. Tell him what you know about the east and west coasts from a cultural and geographical perspective, which area you like more, and why.

3. E-Mail Response

Read this e-mail from a friend and then type a response.

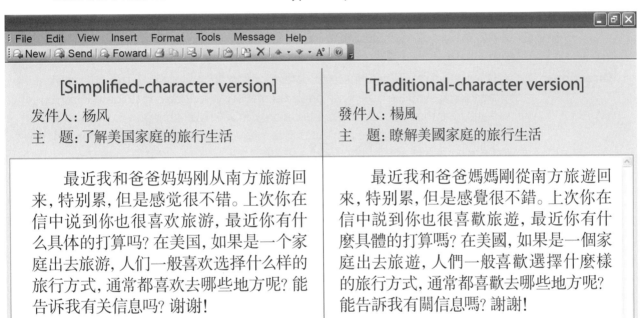

| File Edit View Insert Format Tools Message Help |
| New Send Foward |

[Simplified-character version]	[Traditional-character version]
发件人: 杨风 主　题: 了解美国家庭的旅行生活	發件人: 楊風 主　題: 瞭解美國家庭的旅行生活
最近我和爸爸妈妈刚从南方旅游回来, 特别累, 但是感觉很不错。上次你在信中说到你也很喜欢旅游, 最近你有什么具体的打算吗? 在美国, 如果是一个家庭出去旅游, 人们一般喜欢选择什么样的旅行方式, 通常都喜欢去哪些地方呢? 能告诉我有关信息吗? 谢谢!	最近我和爸爸媽媽剛從南方旅遊回來, 特別累, 但是感覺很不錯。上次你在信中說到你也很喜歡旅遊, 最近你有什麼具體的打算嗎? 在美國, 如果是一個家庭出去旅遊, 人們一般喜歡選擇什麼樣的旅行方式, 通常都喜歡去哪些地方呢? 能告訴我有關信息嗎? 謝謝!

4. Relay a Telephone Message

Imagine you arrive home one day and listen to a message for your sister from her classmate. You will listen twice to the message. Then relay the message, including the important details, by typing a note to your sister.

II. Free Response (Speaking)

Note: In this part, you may NOT move back and forth among questions.

Directions: You will participate in a simulated conversation. Each time it is your turn to speak, you will have 20 seconds to record. You should respond as fully and as appropriately as possible.

1. Conversation

You run into a tourist who just arrived in your hometown. You will have a conversation with him about your hometown.

Directions: You will be asked to speak in Chinese on different topics in the following two questions. In each case, imagine you are making an oral presentation to your class in Chinese. First, you will read and hear the topic for your presentation. You will have 4 minutes to prepare your presentation. Then you will have 2 minutes to record your presentation. Your presentation should be as complete as possible.

2. Cultural Presentation

In your presentation, talk about what you know about the Palace Museum. If you have been there before, include your personal experience as well.

3. Event Plan

Imagine your school and a Chinese school become sister schools. You have the opportunity to plan activities for the students from the sister school during an exchange trip to the United States. In your presentation, explain activities you will arrange for them both on campus and off campus. Also mention your plans for accommodation and meals, and include the reasons for your arrangements.

Answer Sheets

(for Section One)

UNIT ONE
LESSON 1
Sports and Fitness
Shaolin Kung Fu

Answer Sheets

Name: _____

Section One

I. Multiple Choice (Listen to the dialogs)
Circle your answers.

1.	(A)	(B)	(C)	(D)	5.	(A)	(B)	(C)	(D)
2.	(A)	(B)	(C)	(D)	6.	(A)	(B)	(C)	(D)
3.	(A)	(B)	(C)	(D)	7.	(A)	(B)	(C)	(D)
4.	(A)	(B)	(C)	(D)	8.	(A)	(B)	(C)	(D)

II. Multiple Choice (Listen to the selections)
Write your answers (A, B, C, or D) in the blanks.

1. ( )   2. ( )   3. ( )   4. ( )   5. ( )
6. ( )   7. ( )   8. ( )   9. ( )   10. ( )
11. ( )   12. ( )   13. ( )   14. ( )   15. ( )

III. Multiple Choice (Reading)
Write your answers (A, B, C, or D) in the blanks.

1. ( )   2. ( )   3. ( )   4. ( )   5. ( )
6. ( )   7. ( )   8. ( )   9. ( )   10. ( )
11. ( )   12. ( )   13. ( )   14. ( )   15. ( )
16. ( )   17. ( )   18. ( )   19. ( )   20. ( )
21. ( )   22. ( )   23. ( )   24. ( )   25. ( )
26. ( )   27. ( )   28. ( )

jiā yóu **Workbook 1**

UNIT ONE
LESSON 2

Sports and Fitness
What's Your Favorite Sport?

Answer Sheets

Name: _____

Section One

I. Multiple Choice (Listen to the dialogs)
Circle your answers.

1.	(A)	(B)	(C)	(D)	5.	(A)	(B)	(C)	(D)
2.	(A)	(B)	(C)	(D)	6.	(A)	(B)	(C)	(D)
3.	(A)	(B)	(C)	(D)	7.	(A)	(B)	(C)	(D)
4.	(A)	(B)	(C)	(D)	8.	(A)	(B)	(C)	(D)

II. Multiple Choice (Listen to the selections)
Write your answers (A, B, C, or D) in the blanks.

1. (   )   2. (   )   3. (   )   4. (   )   5. (   )

6. (   )   7. (   )   8. (   )   9. (   )   10. (   )

11. (   )   12. (   )   13. (   )   14. (   )

III. Multiple Choice (Reading)
Write your answers (A, B, C, or D) in the blanks.

1. (   )   2. (   )   3. (   )   4. (   )   5. (   )

6. (   )   7. (   )   8. (   )   9. (   )   10. (   )

11. (   )   12. (   )   13. (   )   14. (   )   15. (   )

16. (   )   17. (   )   18. (   )   19. (   )   20. (   )

21. (   )   22. (   )   23. (   )   24. (   )   25. (   )

jiā yóu **Workbook 1**

UNIT TWO
LESSON 3
Food and Fashion
The Beijing Teahouse

Answer Sheets

Name: _____

Section One

I. Multiple Choice (Listen to the dialogs)
Circle your answers.

1.	(A)	(B)	(C)	(D)	5.	(A)	(B)	(C)	(D)
2.	(A)	(B)	(C)	(D)	6.	(A)	(B)	(C)	(D)
3.	(A)	(B)	(C)	(D)	7.	(A)	(B)	(C)	(D)
4.	(A)	(B)	(C)	(D)	8.	(A)	(B)	(C)	(D)

II. Multiple Choice (Listen to the selections)
Write your answers (A, B, C, or D) in the blanks.

1. (   )   2. (   )   3. (   )   4. (   )   5. (   )

6. (   )   7. (   )   8. (   )   9. (   )   10. (   )

11. (   )   12. (   )   13. (   )   14. (   )   15. (   )

III. Multiple Choice (Reading)
Write your answers (A, B, C, or D) in the blanks.

1. (   )   2. (   )   3. (   )   4. (   )   5. (   )

6. (   )   7. (   )   8. (   )   9. (   )   10. (   )

11. (   )   12. (   )   13. (   )   14. (   )   15. (   )

16. (   )   17. (   )   18. (   )   19. (   )   20. (   )

21. (   )   22. (   )   23. (   )   24. (   )   25. (   )

UNIT TWO
LESSON 4
Food and Fashion
What Should a Bridesmaid Wear?

Answer Sheets

Name: _____

Section One

I. Multiple Choice (Listen to the dialogs)
Circle your answers.

1.	(A)	(B)	(C)	(D)	5.	(A)	(B)	(C)	(D)
2.	(A)	(B)	(C)	(D)	6.	(A)	(B)	(C)	(D)
3.	(A)	(B)	(C)	(D)	7.	(A)	(B)	(C)	(D)
4.	(A)	(B)	(C)	(D)	8.	(A)	(B)	(C)	(D)

II. Multiple Choice (Listen to the selections)
Write your answers (A, B, C, or D) in the blanks.

1. (   )   2. (   )   3. (   )   4. (   )   5. (   )

6. (   )   7. (   )   8. (   )   9. (   )   10. (   )

11. (   )   12. (   )   13. (   )   14. (   )   15. (   )

16. (   )

III. Multiple Choice (Reading)
Write your answers (A, B, C, or D) in the blanks.

1. (   )   2. (   )   3. (   )   4. (   )   5. (   )

6. (   )   7. (   )   8. (   )   9. (   )   10. (   )

11. (   )   12. (   )   13. (   )   14. (   )   15. (   )

16. (   )   17. (   )   18. (   )   19. (   )   20. (   )

21. (   )   22. (   )   23. (   )   24. (   )

jiā yóu **Workbook 1**

UNIT THREE School and Family
LESSON 5 Chinese is Fun!

Answer Sheets

Name: _____

Section One

I. Multiple Choice (Listen to the dialogs)
Circle your answers.

1.	(A)	(B)	(C)	(D)	5.	(A)	(B)	(C)	(D)
2.	(A)	(B)	(C)	(D)	6.	(A)	(B)	(C)	(D)
3.	(A)	(B)	(C)	(D)	7.	(A)	(B)	(C)	(D)
4.	(A)	(B)	(C)	(D)	8.	(A)	(B)	(C)	(D)

II. Multiple Choice (Listen to the selections)
Write your answers (A, B, C, or D) in the blanks.

1. (　　)　　2. (　　)　　3. (　　)　　4. (　　)　　5. (　　)

6. (　　)　　7. (　　)　　8. (　　)　　9. (　　)　　10. (　　)

11. (　　)　　12. (　　)　　13. (　　)

III. Multiple Choice (Reading)
Write your answers (A, B, C, or D) in the blanks.

1. (　　)　　2. (　　)　　3. (　　)　　4. (　　)　　5. (　　)

6. (　　)　　7. (　　)　　8. (　　)　　9. (　　)　　10. (　　)

11. (　　)　　12. (　　)　　13. (　　)　　14. (　　)　　15. (　　)

16. (　　)　　17. (　　)　　18. (　　)　　19. (　　)　　20. (　　)

21. (　　)　　22. (　　)

jiā yóu **Workbook 1**

UNIT THREE
LESSON 6
School and Family
My Father, Laoshe

Answer Sheets

Name: _____

Section One

I. Multiple Choice (Listen to the dialogs)
Circle your answers.

1.	(A)	(B)	(C)	(D)		5.	(A)	(B)	(C)	(D)
2.	(A)	(B)	(C)	(D)		6.	(A)	(B)	(C)	(D)
3.	(A)	(B)	(C)	(D)		7.	(A)	(B)	(C)	(D)
4.	(A)	(B)	(C)	(D)		8.	(A)	(B)	(C)	(D)

II. Multiple Choice (Listen to the selections)
Write your answers (A, B, C, or D) in the blanks.

1. (   )   2. (   )   3. (   )   4. (   )   5. (   )

6. (   )   7. (   )   8. (   )   9. (   )   10. (   )

11. (   )   12. (   )   13. (   )   14. (   )   15. (   )

III. Multiple Choice (Reading)
Write your answers (A, B, C, or D) in the blanks.

1. (   )   2. (   )   3. (   )   4. (   )   5. (   )

6. (   )   7. (   )   8. (   )   9. (   )   10. (   )

11. (   )   12. (   )   13. (   )   14. (   )   15. (   )

16. (   )   17. (   )   18. (   )   19. (   )   20. (   )

21. (   )   22. (   )   23. (   )   24. (   )   25. (   )

UNIT FOUR Festivals and Customs
LESSON 7 Celebrating Chinese New Year

Answer Sheets

Name: _____

Section One

I. Multiple Choice (Listen to the dialogs)
Circle your answers.

1.	(A)	(B)	(C)	(D)	5.	(A)	(B)	(C)	(D)
2.	(A)	(B)	(C)	(D)	6.	(A)	(B)	(C)	(D)
3.	(A)	(B)	(C)	(D)	7.	(A)	(B)	(C)	(D)
4.	(A)	(B)	(C)	(D)	8.	(A)	(B)	(C)	(D)

II. Multiple Choice (Listen to the selections)
Write your answers (A, B, C, or D) in the blanks.

1. (   )   2. (   )   3. (   )   4. (   )   5. (   )

6. (   )   7. (   )   8. (   )   9. (   )   10. (   )

11. (   )   12. (   )   13. (   )   14. (   )

III. Multiple Choice (Reading)
Write your answers (A, B, C, or D) in the blanks.

1. (   )   2. (   )   3. (   )   4. (   )   5. (   )

6. (   )   7. (   )   8. (   )   9. (   )   10. (   )

11. (   )   12. (   )   13. (   )   14. (   )   15. (   )

16. (   )   17. (   )   18. (   )   19. (   )   20. (   )

21. (   )

UNIT FOUR
LESSON 8

Festivals and Customs
Moon Festival

Answer Sheets

Name: _____

Section One

I. Multiple Choice (Listen to the dialogs)
Circle your answers.

1.	(A)	(B)	(C)	(D)	5.	(A)	(B)	(C)	(D)
2.	(A)	(B)	(C)	(D)	6.	(A)	(B)	(C)	(D)
3.	(A)	(B)	(C)	(D)	7.	(A)	(B)	(C)	(D)
4.	(A)	(B)	(C)	(D)	8.	(A)	(B)	(C)	(D)

II. Multiple Choice (Listen to the selections)
Write your answers (A, B, C, or D) in the blanks.

1. (   )   2. (   )   3. (   )   4. (   )   5. (   )

6. (   )   7. (   )   8. (   )   9. (   )   10. (   )

11. (   )   12. (   )

III. Multiple Choice (Reading)
Write your answers (A, B, C, or D) in the blanks.

1. (   )   2. (   )   3. (   )   4. (   )   5. (   )

6. (   )   7. (   )   8. (   )   9. (   )   10. (   )

11. (   )   12. (   )   13. (   )   14. (   )   15. (   )

16. (   )   17. (   )   18. (   )   19. (   )   20. (   )

21. (   )   22. (   )   23. (   )   24. (   )

UNIT FIVE
LESSON 9
Travel and Transportation
Planning a Trip to China

Answer Sheets

Name: _____

Section One

I. Multiple Choice (Listen to the dialogs)
Circle your answers.

1.	(A)	(B)	(C)	(D)		5.	(A)	(B)	(C)	(D)
2.	(A)	(B)	(C)	(D)		6.	(A)	(B)	(C)	(D)
3.	(A)	(B)	(C)	(D)		7.	(A)	(B)	(C)	(D)
4.	(A)	(B)	(C)	(D)		8.	(A)	(B)	(C)	(D)

II. Multiple Choice (Listen to the selections)
Write your answers (A, B, C, or D) in the blanks.

1. (　)　　2. (　)　　3. (　)　　4. (　)　　5. (　)

6. (　)　　7. (　)　　8. (　)　　9. (　)　　10. (　)

11. (　)　　12. (　)

III. Multiple Choice (Reading)
Write your answers (A, B, C, or D) in the blanks.

1. (　)　　2. (　)　　3. (　)　　4. (　)　　5. (　)

6. (　)　　7. (　)　　8. (　)　　9. (　)　　10. (　)

11. (　)　　12. (　)　　13. (　)　　14. (　)　　15. (　)

16. (　)　　17. (　)　　18. (　)　　19. (　)　　20. (　)

21. (　)　　22. (　)

jiā yóu **Workbook 1**

UNIT FIVE
LESSON 10
Travel and Transportation
I Climbed the Great Wall

Answer Sheets

Name: _____

Section One

I. Multiple Choice (Listen to the dialogs)
Circle your answers.

1.	(A)	(B)	(C)	(D)		5.	(A)	(B)	(C)	(D)
2.	(A)	(B)	(C)	(D)		6.	(A)	(B)	(C)	(D)
3.	(A)	(B)	(C)	(D)		7.	(A)	(B)	(C)	(D)
4.	(A)	(B)	(C)	(D)		8.	(A)	(B)	(C)	(D)

II. Multiple Choice (Listen to the selections)
Write your answers (A, B, C, or D) in the blanks.

1. ( )   2. ( )   3. ( )   4. ( )   5. ( )

6. ( )   7. ( )   8. ( )   9. ( )   10. ( )

11. ( )   12. ( )   13. ( )   14. ( )   15. ( )

III. Multiple Choice (Reading)
Write your answers (A, B, C, or D) in the blanks.

1. ( )   2. ( )   3. ( )   4. ( )   5. ( )

6. ( )   7. ( )   8. ( )   9. ( )   10. ( )

11. ( )   12. ( )   13. ( )   14. ( )   15. ( )

16. ( )   17. ( )   18. ( )   19. ( )   20. ( )

21. ( )   22. ( )   23. ( )   24. ( )

jiā yóu **Workbook 1**